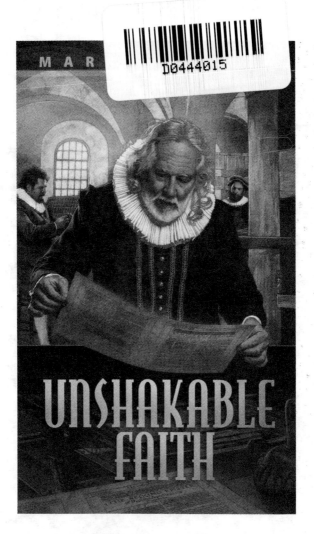

MAR

UNSHAKABLE FAITH

Pacific Press®
Publishing Association

Nampa, Idaho | Oshawa, Ontario, Canada
www.pacificpress.com

Cover design by Gerald Lee Monks
Cover illustration: "Printing the Word" by Nathan Greene,
© 2011, All Rights Reserved,
Used By Permission www.nathangreene.com
Inside design by Kristin Hansen-Mellish

The author assumes full responsibility for the accuracy of all
facts and quotations as cited in this book.

You can obtain additional copies of this book
by calling toll-free 1-800-765-6955 or
by visiting http://www.adventistbookcenter.com.

ISBN: 978-0-8163-6323-0

July 2017

Contents

A Personal Message From Mark Finley

As I wrote this manuscript, I was deeply moved by the stories of men and women who courageously stood for Christ under seemingly insurmountable odds. They were tortured, hunted like wild animals, falsely accused, imprisoned, burned at the stake, and brutally executed. In spite of the injustices they suffered, they remained faithful to Christ. They had a positive, unshakable faith.

What was the source of their inner strength? How did they thrive in such life-threatening conditions? What gave them such courage? Come with me on a journey of discovery. We will travel together to the magnificent Alpine mountains of northern Italy and southern France to meet the Waldenses and marvel at their death-defying faith. We will journey back over the centuries and recapture the living faith of European reformers in the Middle Ages. We will cross the Atlantic and return to America to examine a last-day revival built on the foundation of these Bible-believing Christians.

In reading their stories, you will be inspired by their courage, strengthened by their commitment, and encouraged by their hope. Discovering the secret of their unshakable faith will strengthen your own faith and enable you to thrive in the tough times ahead. This book is about people like you and me who faced challenging circumstances and triumphed through the power of the living Christ. As you read these pages, let Jesus speak to your heart and experience the marvels of His life-transforming grace.

Chapter 1

Light Shines Through Darkness

As I slowly trudged up the narrow, winding Alpine trail in northern Italy, the majesty of the mountains, the pure, fresh mountain air, the flower-filled fields, and the crystal-clear rushing brooks invigorated my spirits. I paused to take in the awe-inspiring views, and my mind drifted back over the centuries. Nearly six hundred years ago, a pilgrim band of weary, chilled-to-the-bone, hungry men, women, and children hastily fled from their medieval oppressors over this same trail.

History calls this period the Dark or Middle Ages. The thirteenth century was not friendly to those who conscientiously opposed the views of the popular church. They were oppressed, persecuted, and butchered in the name of religion. They found refuge in these mountain meadows, rocky crevices, and dark caves. I felt an attraction to these godly people of such stalwart conviction. In the face of insurmountable odds they had a death-defying faith. They stood unflinchingly for what they believed and were willing to sacrifice their very lives for it.

They had something that the twenty-first century so desperately needs—a purpose to live for. Renowned American psychologist Philip Cushman, in his book *Constructing the Self, Constructing America*, discusses people living purposeless lives in a prosperous, self-centered Western individualistic society. He writes of those who have constructed a self that is fundamentally a disappointment to self. Their beliefs are shallow. Little of real significance matters, and they have nothing worth dying for, so they have little worth living for. The force that drives them is an immediate need for self-gratification that ultimately leaves them empty and unsatisfied.

But the men, women, and children whose footprints I followed up this steep, rocky trail were dramatically different. They had an abiding purpose in life. Their beliefs mattered to them, and they were not willing to compromise their integrity. Their core beliefs were part of their spiritual DNA. To deny these beliefs was to deny their identity. In the face of death itself, they had an inner peace. Theirs was a serenity of soul deep within that is absent in our twenty-first-century world of glitz, glamour, and immediate self-gratification. They lived with the certainty that their lives were in the hands of God and He was big enough to handle any problem they might face. Come with me on a journey of discovery as we learn more about these people called the Waldensians.

Who were the Waldensians?

As the spiritual darkness in medieval Europe deepened

and the popular church drifted further away from biblical teachings, false doctrines held minds hostage. The masses were consumed with guilt. They viewed God as a wrathful tyrant and vindictive judge who needed to be appeased rather than a loving God who cared for them and longed for their affection.

At this critical juncture of human history, God began to raise up spiritual seekers who would lead men and women out of spiritual darkness into the light of God's Word. One of these spiritual seekers was a man named Peter Waldo, who was born in Lyons, France in A.D. 1140. He was the leader of a group of Bible-believing Christians who later became known as the Waldenses. His teachings were like a breath of fresh air. Hope rose in human hearts. The shackles that bound men and women for so long were broken.

Peter Waldo believed that the Bible was the basis of all faith, the foundation of truth, and an infallible guide for all believers. He rejected the notion that the Bible must be interpreted by the church to be understood, and he taught that the average person could read and understand the Bible for themselves. Waldo is credited with providing Europe with the first translation of the Bible in a language besides Latin. The Waldenses were powerful witnesses to the life-changing power of the Bible and its transformative influence in daily living. They discovered light for their darkness in the Word of God. They accepted it as the divinely inspired authority for their lives. Its teachings buoyed their spirits, encouraged their hearts, and brought joy to their souls.

Rediscovering the Word of God

Is it possible that a rediscovery of the teachings of the Word of God could give us new purpose for living in the twenty-first century? Does this ancient book have anything significant to say to us? Does its message still speak to seeking hearts today? Is the Bible divinely inspired or is it merely a collection of human ideas about life?

What we believe about the Bible makes a dramatic difference in how we live our lives. If the Bible is simply a collection of human ideas, then we can accept it or reject it with little eternal consequence. But if the Bible is the divinely inspired Word of God, neglecting its teachings has eternal consequences. The Waldenses accepted the inspiration of the Word of God by faith. Does it stand up to the scrutiny of modern scholarship? Is there evidence that it is divinely inspired? Let's consider some of the evidence.

Claims of inspiration

Here is one critical fact: the Bible claims to be inspired. It uses expressions like "and God said" or "the Lord spoke" more than three thousand times. The apostle Paul, in speaking to his young colleague Timothy, declared, "All Scripture is given by inspiration of God" (2 Timothy 3:16). Peter adds, "Holy men of God spoke as they were moved by the Holy Spirit" (2 Peter 1:21).

Let's suppose it is not true that the Bible is inspired by God. What implications would this have, since the Bible so forthrightly claims that it is inspired by God? If it were not inspired, it seems that there would be one of two alternatives. One option is that those who claimed to be inspired were openly lying. They knew their claim to inspiration was false and they stated it anyway, with the express purpose of deceiving people with the claim that their words conveyed a special authority. The other option might be that those who wrote the Bible thought they were inspired but were not. In other words, they were deluded. If either of these presuppositions were true, how could the Bible possibly have such power to change millions of lives? How could its moral claims be so eloquently stated? How could its prophecies be so accurate and the archeological evidence for its truthfulness be so convincing?

The only logical conclusion for thinking minds who carefully examine the evidence is that the Bible is everything it claims to be. Let's examine some of the evidence.

Fulfilled prophecy

J. Barton Payne's *Encyclopedia of Biblical Prophecy* lists 1,239 prophecies in the Old Testament and 578 prophecies in the New Testament—a total of 1,817 prophecies in the entire Bible. These prophecies are meticulously detailed. They deal with entire nations, specific cities, political leaders, definite dates, whole empires, the coming of the Messiah, and last-day events. Throughout the millennia, the fulfillment of these prophecies has testified to their uncanny accuracy. The Bible is unique in both the scope, number, and detailed nature of its predictions.

Speaking of God's ability to foretell the future, the prophet Isaiah declares, "Remember the former things of old. For I am God and there is no other; I am God and there is none like me, declaring the end from the beginning, and declaring from ancient times the things not yet done" (Isaiah 46:9, 10, ESV). One of the strongest evidences of the divine inspiration of the Bible is the fulfillment of its predictions. In fact, Jesus said, "And I have told you before it comes, that when it does come to pass, you may believe" (John 14:29). Jesus' words are too plain to be misunderstood. The function of fulfilled prophecy is to confirm our belief in the integrity and inspiration of Scripture. It is provided so we will believe.

Here are just a few examples of the precision and accuracy of Bible prophecy. There are multiple prophecies that forecast specific events in the life of Christ. Seven hundred years before His birth, the prophet Micah predicted He would be born in Bethlehem (Micah 5:2). It is no accident that a decree of Caesar Augustus brought Mary and Joseph from their hometown of Nazareth more than ninety miles to Bethlehem before Jesus' birth, in exact fulfillment of Micah's prophecy. But the predictions do not end there. Isaiah predicted He would be born of a virgin (Isaiah 7:14). The psalmist David predicted the Messiah would be crucified (Psalm 22:16). And Zechariah declared He would be betrayed by a friend for thirty pieces of silver (Zechariah 11:12, 13).

Some of the most fascinating prophecies of the Bible deal with nations and entire empires. Jeremiah predicted that the ancient, mighty city of Babylon would be destroyed and never rebuilt. Here are the prophet's words: "Babylon shall become a heap, a dwelling place for jackals, an astonishment and a hissing, without an inhabitant" (Jeremiah 51:37). Many cities throughout history have been destroyed by the ravages of war—think of the cities destroyed in World War II, like London, Frankfurt, and many others. But each of these has been rebuilt, and they are thriving cities today. Babylon was overthrown by the Persian armies, and it has never been rebuilt. Alexander the Great employed ten thousand men to rebuild the city of Babylon, but the project was abandoned when he died suddenly. Cyrus, the Persian general who led the attack on Babylon, was named in Bible prophecy nearly 150 years before Babylon's overthrow (Isaiah 44:28; 45:1, 2). And Alexander the Great's Greek empire was specifically named by the prophet Daniel as the nation that would overthrow the Medes and Persians (Daniel 8:20, 21) at least fifteen years before the event. The windswept sands of time forcefully speak of the accuracy of the Bible's predictions.

It would take a quantum leap of faith to believe that these predictions were fulfilled by chance. The mathematical possibility that each of these predicted events took place by some random accident is too large to be imagined. Fulfilled prophecy reveals the accuracy of Bible prophecy and confirms the inspiration of Scripture.

Archeology testifies

Recent discoveries in archeology help to verify numerous people and places mentioned in the Bible, giving us another link in the chain of evidence pointing to divine inspiration. For example, the discovery of the Dead Sea Scrolls at Qumran in 1947 that match closely with various other Bible texts helps to build our confidence that the Bible manuscripts were copied accurately. The Moabite Stone, discovered in 1868 in Jordan, confirms the Old Testament story of the Moabite attacks on Israel as recorded in the first and third chapters of 2 Kings. This is hard evidence from outside the Bible of a specific event recorded by the writers of Scripture. The Lachish Letters, discovered in 1935, about twenty-five miles north of Beersheba, describe the attack of Nebuchadnezzar on Jerusalem in 586 B.C. Carefully chronicling the fall of Jerusalem, they reveal the attack from the perspective of the ancient pagan forces hostile to God. And at Tel Dan in northern Israel, the discovery of the Tel Dan Stele confirms David as the king of Israel.

The Bible mentions a people called the Hittites forty-eight times, discussing their dealings with Abraham, David, and Solomon. These biblical references picture the Hittites as a powerful ancient empire. Yet for centuries, in all the records of antiquity outside of the Bible, not a trace of them was evident. Scholarly critics reasoned that it would be impossible for such a mighty empire to disappear from the pages of history without leaving a single trace behind. This lack of evidence outside the Bible was taken to mean that the Hittites never existed. Then came the discovery of the Rosetta Stone, which contained writing in Egyptian and Greek. When the brilliant French scholar Jean-François Champollion deciphered the hieroglyphics, he unlocked the mystery of the ancient picture-writing of the Egyptians. Centuries-old monuments now spoke and revealed that the Hittites did in fact exist, that they were the powerful nation the Bible describes, battling against the Egyptians. Today no credible scholar in the world who has examined the facts harbors doubt about the existence of the Hittites.

Additionally, the name of Pontius Pilate discovered in Caesarea, along with the family tomb of Caiaphas found outside of Jerusalem, are powerful testimonies of key players in the crucifixion story. Each year further discoveries in archeology confirm the accuracy and reliability of the Bible. These discoveries speak of a God who has not left Himself without a witness in this world.

Life-transforming power

Millions around the world testify to the changes in their lives as a result of their Bible study. The Bible's appeal is both universal and eternal. Its message speaks to people of all ages, to all ethnic groups, and to all cultures in all generations.

Through reading the Bible, drunkards become sober, thieves become honest, prostitutes become pure, and drug addicts become clean. Anger, bitterness, and resentment yield to loving forgiveness, mercy, and graciousness. Selfish greed gives way to unselfish service. Crumbling marriages are rebuilt. Broken relationships are rekindled. Shattered self-esteem is restored. In God's Word, the weak find strength, the guilty find forgiveness, the discouraged find new joy, and the despairing find hope. The same Holy Spirit who inspired the Bible writers inspires those who read it.

An unshakable faith

Recognizing the life-changing power of the Word of God, the Waldenses spent countless hours teaching its principles to their children. When still in their teens the Waldensian young people memorized the Gospels of

Matthew and John. They copied their precious manu-scripts, hid them in their long flowing robes, left their quiet mountain retreats posed as merchants or students, and traveled to the great cities and universities of Europe. When they were providentially brought into contact with honest seekers, they quietly shared their precious Bible manuscripts. Some of them enrolled as students in Europe's leading universities, and as the Holy Spirit opened the doors of opportunity they shared the truths of God's Word.

Light penetrated the darkness. Hope blossomed. Faith replaced doubt. A sense of Christ's presence ban-ished fear. The joy of forgiveness, like a refreshing rain after the drought of summer, brought new life to their parched souls. This small group of faithful Waldensian Christians refused to accept the decrees of the state-sponsored church in place of the Word of God. For them, the teachings of the Word of God were far more important than the time-worn traditions of formal re-ligion. The state-sponsored church responded with an all-out effort to destroy the so-called heretics.

The trail of tears

As I hiked in the beauty of the mountains over the same trail that the Waldenses used centuries ago, my mind turned to their sufferings and undaunted faith. One spring morning, high on a mountain, the Waldensi-ans heard shouting far below as Colonel DePerot, the military officer assigned to stamp them out, and his forces prepared to attack them. Pointing to the top of the mountains where the Waldensians were camped, he boasted, "My lads, we shall sleep up there tonight." He invited the villagers in the valleys to a public hanging to take place the next day. "Come and see the end of the Waldensians," he proclaimed.

High atop the peak, Waldensian leader Henri Arnaud opened his Bible and read to his company from Psalm 124:2, 3: "If it had not been the Lord who was on our side, when men rose up against us, then they would have swallowed us alive."

DePerot and his troops started up the mountain. All went well until the best climbers were ready to reach the timbers of the mountain fort. At that point, Arnaud's men hailed a volley of stones upon them. The troops fell back. Colonel DePerot was wounded and had to request refuge in the Waldensian fort. The Waldensians graciously gave him a place to sleep for the night. On the next night, DePerot's soldiers thought they had surrounded the fort, but the Waldensians slipped away through the fog on a secret trail higher into the mountains. Recognizing that the Waldensians had slipped away, one of DePerot's men is reported to have said, "Heaven seems to take a special interest in preserving these people."

At other times, many Waldensians were martyred for their faith. They languished in dark, damp, dingy prisons. They were hurled from the mountain heights. They were butchered and burned at the stake. But the truth they so valiantly stood for penetrated the darkness. They accepted martyrdom rather than surrender their faith.

The witness of these faithful martyrs calls us to loyalty. Their testimony appeals to us to make an unwavering commitment to God. The legacy of their lives speaks to us in this easy-going, compromising age. God is calling this generation to a deeper commitment. He is calling us to an uncompromising faith, to a steadfast loyalty to His Word. Are there areas of compromise in your personal life? Have your values been shaped by the culture around you? Have you compromised your integrity and lost a real sense of the moral principles that govern your life? Are there some things you feel uncomfortable about doing but not so uncomfortable that you stop doing them?

The stalwart faith of the Waldensians echoes down the corridors of time. The unshakable faith of these heroes of yesterday speaks to our hearts today. They lived in another time and another place, but the witness of their lives speaks to us wherever we are in every generation. Today, why not determine again, by God's grace, to be faithful until He comes? In the blazing light of eternity, why not commit your life to living by the principles in God's Word? If you make this commitment, you will discover the peace and purpose of the Waldensians along whatever trail you walk and wherever life takes you on its journey of faith.

Chapter 2

Standing for the Word

In June of A.D. 1348 an English seaman arrived in Weymouth from southwest France with some strange symptoms. He was running a high fever, experiencing chills, and feeling extremely weak. In a few days he developed large boil-like swellings in his lymph node areas; and his nose, hands, and feet blackened. The Black Death had arrived in England.

The Black Death was carried by flea-infested rats from Asia aboard sailing vessels. By October the plague had reached London, and by the summer of 1349 it had spread through the entire country. This dreaded disease devastated the nation. Conservative estimates indicate that at least 30 percent of the population died, and some researchers believe the figure was closer to 60 percent. The economy suffered because of the obliterated work-force. Wages skyrocketed for the remaining few workers.

The wealthy landowners reacted strongly to this increase in wages. This led to a clash between the rich and the poor, between the well-to-do aristocrats and the peasant workers. The Peasants' Revolt of 1381 was largely the result of the resentment of the working class over the landowner's insistence on lower wages. These were turbulent times of social upheaval, uncertainty, and spiritual darkness. Monks appealed to the poor populace for lavish offerings, promising them absolution for sin and guaranteeing them eternity. The church degenerated into a hollow shell of spiritual life locked in the ritual of formal religion. It was devoid of spiritual power. The stifling stranglehold of ritual destroyed all genuine faith. With the poor economic conditions, social upheaval, waning support for the arts, and spiritual confusion, men and women seemed lost in a dense fog of uncertainty.

The religious drama deepened. The papacy was not in Rome, the eternal city, but in Avignon, under the control of the French. Although the French domination of the church came to an end in the mid-fourteenth century, it ended with the papal schism during which there were two popes, and sometimes three, in conflict with one another. Each one mobilized their armies against the other and placed their rival under the curse of Satan. The average person was bewildered about these battles in the name of religion. A spiritual darkness settled over the land. Thousands lost hope of a bright future. It was at this critical point in the history of England that John Wycliffe appeared upon the scene.

England's spiritual longings

England was a difficult place in which to live during Wycliffe's life. Emphasis on education increased, and the road to success led through the colleges. However, few people had enough money to attend college, and the lot of the peasant was difficult and spiritually empty. The peasants were largely dependent on the friars for their religious instruction. The friars' sermons were sensational and emotional but lacked any biblical substance. The average person may have known a little about the sayings of Christ and a few of the more familiar Bible stories but not much of anything else. They did not have access to the Bible. Even if they were fortunate enough to see a copy chained to some monastery wall, they could not read or understand it. God raised up John Wycliffe to change the history of Christianity in both England and the Western world.

John Wycliffe: A brilliant scholar

John Wycliffe was born sometime in the mid 1320s. From his earliest years he was an outstanding student who diligently pursued every opportunity to study. At college he was noted for his brilliant mind, diligent study habits, and sound scholarship. He was educated in philosophy, civil law, and the traditions and history of the church. While Wycliffe was still a college student, he entered upon a careful study of the Scriptures. He passionately pored over the teachings of Scripture hour after hour. The more he studied God's Word, the more he sensed the leading of the Holy Spirit. His heart warmed. He found answers to questions that had loomed large in his mind for decades. His spiritual thirst was quenched at the fountain of God's Word. And his spiritual hunger was satisfied by the "spiritual bread" from heaven. "In the Word of God he found that which he had before sought in vain. Here he saw the plan of salvation revealed and Christ set forth as the only advocate for man. He gave himself to the service of Christ and determined to proclaim the truths he had discovered."[1]

Professor of theology/biblical preacher

Eventually Wycliffe became a professor of theology at Oxford University and preached the Word of God in the halls of the university. His students were thrilled with his clear exposition of the Scriptures. The instruction in the epistle of James spoke to these students' hearts. "Therefore lay aside all filthiness and overflow of wickedness, and receive with meekness the implanted word, which is able to save your souls" (James 1:21). The "implanted word" changed their lives. Spiritual renewal took place. Oxford University became the center of biblical preaching in all of England as Wycliffe became a mighty champion for the Word of God. When the Word of God is studied with an open mind and receptive heart, the Holy Spirit speaks through it to change people's lives. It certainly changed Wycliffe's life and the lives of the students who listened to him preach.

The same Holy Spirit who inspired the Bible in the first place inspires those who read it and honestly accept its instruction in their own lives. There is life-changing power in the Word of God. Wycliffe experienced this power in his own life. He was a man of sterling character and utmost integrity. He discovered that the prayerful study of the Scriptures gives a stability of purpose, indomitable courage, and an enduring fortitude, strength of intellect, and depth of moral conviction. His teachings affected not only his university students but also every segment of society, from poverty-stricken peasants to wealthy aristocrats, from shopkeepers to farmers, from dockhands to royalty, from merchants to academics. It seemed that all of England was moved by the powerful preaching and teaching of John Wycliffe. If one man could change a nation's spiritual direction and destiny, John Wycliffe did it.

Wycliffe's teachings

Wycliffe placed emphasis on three cardinal beliefs. First, he believed and preached that the Bible was the sole authority in spiritual matters. Wycliffe taught that the Bible is the perfect revelation of God's will. He had implicit faith in the inspired truth of Scripture and preached that it provides the foundation for all faith. He emphasized that Christ speaking through His Word was more important than any earthly leader speaking through church councils. Second, he taught that the Holy Spirit is the infallible interpreter of the Bible, not priests or prelates or popes (2 Peter 1:21; John 16:7, 8). Third, he taught the all-sufficiency and life-changing power of the Word as a revelation of Christ (2 Peter 1:4). Christ became all in all for Wycliffe. Jesus was the essence of his faith, the heart of his proclamation, and the center of all of his teaching. For Wycliffe the message of the Bible was life giving. It was the foundation of all true spirituality.

Wycliffe's life goal

It is then quite understandable that the goal of Wycliffe's life was to translate the Bible into the language of the

English-speaking peoples. The burden of his heart and his overwhelming desire was to translate the Bible into understandable, everyday English so everyone from the average person on the street to the professor in the university could read it. For years he tirelessly labored to accomplish this task. When his work was completed at an immense personal sacrifice and great toll on his own health, he felt satisfied that his lifework was over. He did not fear prison, torture, or martyrdom. He had placed the Scriptures in the hands of the English-speaking people, and he knew that the light of God's Word would never be extinguished. Truth would prevail over falsehood. The Word of God would triumph over tradition. The light of Scripture would illumine the darkness and light the path to eternal life.

Wycliffe was often sick because of overwork. It seems he was constantly teaching, preaching, and writing. He was under constant pressure from the popular church to compromise his integrity and conform to the teachings of the church. His conscience would not allow him to compromise his convictions and place a human being at the head of the church rather than the living Christ. He was tried for his faith, condemned as a heretic, and placed under the sentence of death. At his trial Wycliffe spoke eloquently of the authority of the Scriptures and exposed the hypocrisy and sins of the medieval church leaders. Although church and state united against him, he made this earnest appeal: "With whom think you are ye contending? with an old man on the brink of the grave? No! With Truth—Truth which is stronger than you, and will overcome you."[2]

He was condemned by the church, but before he could be prosecuted, he died of a stroke on New Year's Eve in 1384. His memory and influence continued to be so strong that he was formally condemned again thirty years later at the Council of Constance. Orders were given for his writings to be destroyed, his bones exhumed and burned, and the ashes to be thrown into the nearby river. Somehow the church authorities thought that by burning his remains they might erase his memory. But even such bizarre and extreme actions could not stop the hunger for God's Word and truth, for which Wycliffe had uncompromisingly advocated, from moving the masses in England. One English writer put it this way: "[They] burnt [his bones] to ashes, and cast them into the Swift, a neighbouring brook running hard by. Thus this brook hath conveyed his ashes into Avon, Avon into Severn; Severn into the narrow seas; they into the main ocean; and thus the ashes of Wicliffe are the emblem of his doctrine, which now is dispersed all the world over."[3]

Wycliffe's greatest contribution, the translation of the English Bible, would be his enduring legacy to Christianity. All of Wycliffe's Bibles were copied by hand. The art of printing was still unknown. Johannes Gutenberg would not invent moveable type until seventy years later, and the first copies of the Bible would not come off his press until the 1450s. The slow and laborious task of hand copying the Scriptures was practiced down through the ages. Scribes carefully copied the Word of God in what we would classify as very primitive conditions. There were no computers, high-speed presses, or digital photocopying machines. Without modern technology, the only option to preserve the sacred word of God was for scribes to copy it by hand.

Copying accuracy

Since the Bible was hand copied for centuries, can we be sure of its accuracy? What guarantees that the Bible we hold in our hands today contains the same inspired message as when it was originally written? Have there been dramatic changes in its content? Who copied the Bible, and how careful were they when they copied its pages?

The discovery of the Dead Sea Scrolls in 1947 was one of the most significant and providential finds in the history of archeology. The initial discovery by Bedouin shepherds (who were also cousins) Khalil Musa, Jum'a Muhammed Khalil, and Muhammed Ahmed el-Hamed (nicknamed edh-Dhib) confirms the integrity of the copying process. On a sweltering hot summer day in the arid Judean desert, not far from the Dead Sea, the three Bedouin shepherd boys were hunting for a lost sheep. Jum'a threw a stone into a cave where he thought the sheep might have wandered, to scare it out. To his surprise, he heard the breaking of pottery. He immediately thought of hidden treasure. Edh-Dhib was the first to actually climb into one of the caves. On the floor of the cave were several jars containing leather scrolls wrapped in linen cloth and some broken pottery. He retrieved a handful of scrolls and took them back to the Bedouin camp to show to his family.

The Bedouins returned and searched the cave. They discovered seven scrolls housed in jars. None of the scrolls were destroyed in this process, despite some published reports that say they were. The Bedouin carefully guarded this amazing find until they determined what to do with the scrolls. Eventually they took the scrolls to a so-called antiquities dealer in Bethlehem, who returned them, saying they were worthless. Undaunted, the Bedouin went to a nearby market, where a Syrian Christian offered to buy them. A sheikh joined their conversation and suggested they take the scrolls to Khalil Eskander Shahin, known as Kando, a cobbler and part-time antiques dealer. The Bedouin and the dealers returned to the site, leaving one scroll with Kando and selling three others to a dealer for the equivalent of about twenty-eight dollars. Can you imagine one of the greatest finds in archeological history being deemed worthless and selling for so little? There is a spiritual lesson here. Some still consider the Scriptures to be of little value when they are holding the most valuable treasure in their hands.

The original scrolls continued to change hands until eventually they came into the possession of Hebrew University in Jerusalem. After examining the scrolls, Professor E. L. Sukenik made this remarkable statement in his diary: "It may be that this is one of the greatest finds ever made in Palestine, a find we had never so much as hoped for." More scrolls were discovered after the seven original scrolls, and today we have manuscripts of every book of the Old Testament with the possible exception of Ruth. Some of the manuscripts like Isaiah contain the entire Bible book, and others only fragments or parts of a Bible book. The Isaiah Scroll is complete and measures twenty-four feet long and ten inches high.

The Dead Sea Scrolls date back two thousand years to the first century before Christ. They are the oldest manuscripts of the Bible in existence. They consist of more than forty thousand handwritten fragments, and more than five hundred books have been pieced together from these manuscripts.

The copyists

Archeological digs in the area of the caves revealed the existence of an Essene community at Qumran, not far from the Dead Sea, complete with its scriptorium for copying ancient manuscripts. The Essenes were conservative Jews who loathed the laxness and liberality of the priests in Jerusalem. They spent a lifetime copying ancient Bible manuscripts and Jewish community rules of faith, ritual, and tradition. Their copying rules were extremely strict. Specially trained scribes were educated to reproduce the Scriptures. They preserved their sacred book as no other book in history has been preserved. They accounted for every letter, syllable, word, and paragraph.

The significance of the Dead Sea Scrolls cannot be overestimated. They provide firsthand evidence that the Bible has been accurately copied throughout the centuries. We can compare the Dead Sea Scrolls with later manuscripts and critically observe that there are no major differences in the text of Scripture.

Most of the Old Testament was written in Hebrew, while a small portion was written in Aramaic. Centuries before the time of Jesus, Judaism already had developed the practice of carefully preserving the Scriptures. The Jewish scribes held the Word of God in such high esteem that they regarded the copying of any error as a sin. No imperfection, no matter how small, was tolerated. The successors to this meticulous scribal tradition were Jewish biblical scholars known as the Masoretes.

The amazing story of the Masoretes

The Masoretes copied the Bible between A.D. 700 and 800. Their copies were made nearly one thousand years after the copies in the Dead Sea Scrolls. They developed a thorough system of checks to ensure that every copy was accurate. To make certain they had not added or left out even a single letter, they counted the number of times each letter of the alphabet occurred in each book. They noted and recorded the middle letter of the entire Old Testament. They recorded the middle letter on each page and the number of letters and words in each column. They examined every copy of the Old Testament and withdrew from circulation all copies in which any error was discovered.

These carefully copied Hebrew texts were virtually identical to the Scriptural texts in the Dead Sea Scrolls. In other words, you can take copies of Isaiah in the Dead Sea Scrolls and compare them with the Masoretic copies made nearly one thousand years later and find no essential difference. Just as God inspired the authors who wrote the Word of God, He guided the copyists who faithfully and diligently copied it.

The story of the Bible's copying gets even more complex. One source puts it this way: "Numbers were placed at the end of each book, telling the copyists the exact number of words that a book contained in its original manuscript. If the copy had a few more words or a few less words than the original, the copy was thrown away. At the end of each book, the Masoretes also listed the word or the phrase that would have numerically been found in the exact middle of the book. Again, if the copy did not have the right word or phrase in its middle, it was thrown away."[4]

For accuracy, the scribes checked one another's work. After one scribe finished copying a book of the Bible, another scribe would count the words and also look for that key phrase in the middle of the book. If the second scribe found no mistakes, the copy could be kept and used. If he found a single error, or found that the key phrase was not in the exact middle of the book, he would throw away the copy. All of that work would have been for nothing.

How would you like to have been a Bible copyist and work for months copying the entirety of a Bible book only to make a few mistakes and have your entire work discarded? A scribe could spend several months copying an entire section of the Bible, only to find that he was one word off and had to see his work put in the trash.

The 1947 discovery of the Dead Sea Scrolls provided biblical linguists, translators, archeologists, and theologians the opportunity to compare the biblical manuscripts found at Qumran with the Masoretic text that was copied approximately one thousand years later, in the eighth and ninth centuries. When compared to these ancient copies, the Masoretic texts were found to be so close to identical that Bible scholar W. F. Albright emphatically declared, "We may rest assured that the consonantal text of the Hebrew Bible, though not infallible, has been preserved with an accuracy perhaps unparalleled in any other Near-Eastern literature."[5] Sir Frederic Kenyon added, "The Christian can take the whole Bible in his hand and say without fear or hesitation that he holds in it the true Word of God, faithfully handed down from generation to generation throughout the centuries."[6] There is more manuscript evidence testifying to the accurate copying of the Bible than any other single ancient manuscript. Based on the available twenty-first-century evidence, we can trust the Bible. It is the reliable, authoritative, inspired revelation of God's will for mankind. John Wycliffe's assertion of the authority of Scripture and its revelation of God's will has proven true through the centuries.

The Bible: A universal book

Wycliffe's influence still lives on today. In 1942 the Wycliffe Bible Translators organization was founded. The purpose of the Wycliffe translators was to provide the Bible to people groups that did not have it readily available in their own language. They were committed to carry on the dream of John Wycliffe to give people the Bible in their mother tongue. The organization completed its first translation of the Bible in 1951, and fifty years later, in 2000, completed the five-hundredth translation. Around the same time, the Wycliffe organization adopted a new challenge—the goal of starting, by 2025, a Bible translation project in every language that still needs one.

Today, as a result of the faithful work of the Wycliffe

Bible Translators and other international Bible translation organizations both large and small, people of more than 1,400 languages have access to the New Testament and some other portions of Scripture in their language. More than six hundred languages have the complete translated Bible. More than 2,400 languages across 130 countries have active translation and linguistic development work happening right now. John Wycliffe's life is a testimony to the truthfulness of Jesus' declaration, "Heaven and earth will pass away, but My words will by no means pass away" (Matthew 24:35). Wycliffe would also be amazed that Jesus' words, "And this gospel of the kingdom will be preached in all the world as a witness to all nations, and then the end will come" (Matthew 24:14) are being fulfilled in this generation. Wycliffe's accusers and persecutors have long since perished, but the truth he lived and died for still lives on. It is still changing lives. It is still having an impact on towns, villages, cities, and entire continents. It is still making a difference in tens of thousands of lives, and it will make a difference in the lives of all who read it prayerfully and let its divinely inspired words change their lives. The Bible does us little good if it rests on the shelves of our homes, unread, but if it lodges in our hearts, it changes our lives.

---

1. Ellen G. White, *The Great Controversy* (Mountain View, CA: Pacific Press®, 1911), 81.

2. J. A. Wylie, *The History of Protestantism*, 1:123.

3. Thomas Fuller, *The Church History of Britain*, 2:424.

4. Jeremy Cagle, "Was the Bible Copied Accurately?" *Just the Simple Truth* (blog), accessed June 15, 2017, http://www

.justthesimpletruth.com/was-the-bible-copied-accurately/.

5. W. F. Albright, "The Old Testament and the Archaeology of Palestine," in H. H. Rowley, ed., *The Old Testament and Modern Study: A Generation of Discovery and Research, Essays by Members of the Society for Old Testament Study* (London: Oxford University Press, 1961), 25.

6. Frederic George Kenyon, *Our Bible and the Ancient Manuscript*, 3rd ed. (London: Eyre and Spottiswoode, 1897), 11.

Chapter 3

Faith in the Flames

Poverty does not shackle people to lifelong destitution. It does not imprison them in ignorance. John Huss was of humble birth, born around A.D. 1369 and left fatherless at a very young age. His devoted mother believed God had better plans for her young son. She continually prayed for him and taught him the eternal principles of the Bible early in life. Her desire was that her son know God, live in harmony with the principles of Scripture, and receive a good education. She understood very early in John's life that God had a special purpose for him. He had an unusually bright mind and developed outstanding communication skills at a very young age.

While still a lad, he and his mother left their native village of Husenic in southern Bohemia and made the arduous journey to Prague. John enrolled in a parish school to get a much more thorough education than was possible in his small country village. As they approached the city, his mother paused on an isolated forest pathway and earnestly prayed. She asked God to keep her son faithful to Him. She prayed that in Prague he would never compromise his commitment to truth.

His mother's prayers were answered. John Huss never wavered from his faithfulness to Christ and His Word. Little did John's mother know as she knelt in the quietness of her forest cathedral that God would use her son to change the world! The young scholar would influence kings and queens, nobles and princes, villagers and farm-workers across an entire continent.

Arriving in Prague, the enterprising and industrious young man supported himself by singing and doing any menial tasks that the priests assigned him. Whatever he did, he did it enthusiastically and thoroughly. Soon he distinguished himself as an outstanding student and a brilliant scholar.

He was eventually admitted to the University of Prague as a charity case and quickly was recognized as one of the university's brightest minds and most diligent students. By 1396, at twenty-seven years old, John Huss, the poverty-stricken, underprivileged boy from an obscure village in Bohemia, graduated from one of Europe's most prestigious universities. Among three thousand students he was at the top of his class. His name was now well known throughout Prague. By the early 1400s, this bright young man became a lecturer at the University of Prague. It was there that events occurred which would change his life and change the world.

Changed by the Word

On one occasion, while poring over manuscripts in the university library, Huss discovered the writings of John

Wycliffe, the English Reformer. Wycliffe's emphasis on the primacy of the Bible, the authority of Scripture, and the centrality of Christ profoundly influenced John Huss. Wycliffe's writings led him to more diligently study the Bible for himself. As he spent hours poring over the Scriptures, he was convinced that the church in Bohemia needed both a spiritual revival and a decided reformation.

Several years after taking his priest orders, he was appointed rector of the Bethlehem Chapel in Prague. The founders of this chapel advocated preaching the Scriptures in the language of the people. He became a powerful preacher renowned throughout Europe; and when he began to preach that many of the church's beliefs could not be reconciled with Scripture, it sent shock waves throughout the church in Europe.

Standing on the authority of the Bible alone, he boldly called for reform in the lives and beliefs of fellow church members. His belief regarding the authority of the Bible can be summed in these words: he was convinced that "the precepts of Scripture, conveyed through the understanding, are to rule the conscience; in other words, that God speaking in the Bible, and not the church speaking through the priesthood, is the one infallible guide."[1] His faith was anchored in the eternal certainty of God's Word, not the changeable human opinions of church leaders, the traditions of the church hierarchy, or changing winds of popular opinion. The Scriptures became the supreme guide of his life and the heart of his preaching and teaching.

Set free by the truth

Christ's words in John's Gospel deeply impressed Huss. Jesus declared, "You shall know the truth, and the truth shall make you free" (John 8:32). Truth is liberating. It frees us from oppressive guilt, the accusing voices of a condemning conscience, and the bondage of sinful habits and practices. The truth about Jesus' love and grace is life transforming. When we understand that God's love is limitless and all of heaven is working for our salvation, it changes our lives.

God took the initiative in our salvation. When Adam and Eve sinned, He did not push this planet off the edge of the universe into oblivion. He did not destroy it and start over. He did not annihilate our first parents. His care for them was too great, and His desire to win back their affection was too strong. He came to the garden in love, seeking His lost children to share with them love's response to their sin and love's answer to human rebellion. With sorrow in His voice and tears in His eyes, the God of the universe cried out, "Adam, where are you?"

Adam and Eve had run *from* their Creator, but He was running *toward* them. They were hiding from Him, but He was searching for them and would not give up until they were found. The God we serve is a seeking God. He takes the initiative. Francis Thompson, the English poet, captures this thought in his remarkable 182-line poem titled, "The Hound of Heaven." In it, he compares the persistence of a hound eagerly chasing a rabbit with God's pursuit of each one of us.

This well-loved Christian poem, "The Hound of Heaven," has been described as follows:

The name is strange. It startles one at first. It is so bold, so new, and so fearless. It does not attract, rather the reverse. But when one reads the poem this strangeness disappears. The meaning is understood. As the hound follows the hare, never ceasing in its running, ever drawing nearer in the chase, with unhurrying and unperturbed pace, so does God follow the fleeing soul by His Divine grace. And though in sin or in human love, away from God it seeks to hide itself, Divine grace follows after, unwearyingly follows ever after, till the soul feels its pressure forcing it to turn to Him alone in that never ending pursuit.[2]

Lost and found

Throughout Scripture, this is the picture of God presented in the Bible—a seeking, pursuing, searching God. He is the Good Shepherd seeking the lost sheep until He finds it (see Luke 15:1–4). He is the woman persistently searching for her lost coin. She will not give up until the entire house is swept clean and she has done everything she can to find her lost silver dowry coin (see Luke 15:5, 6). God is like that. He searches through the rubble to find His lost children, who are much more valuable than a lost coin. He is the heartbroken father who gives his young-adult son the freedom to walk away and daily longs for his return. He will never give up hoping, dreaming, and praying that the son he loves so much will come home. He is the lonely father, who every day waits, eagerly gazing down the road, and longing for the faintest glimpse of his son.

When one day he sees his rebellious boy clothed in tattered rags, his emaciated body slowly making its way home, with his head bowed in guilt and despair, the father is overwhelmed with joy. He cannot hold himself back and runs to meet him, throws his arms around his son, and celebrates his return with a magnificent welcome party.

The God that John Huss discovered was not a harsh judge or an authoritarian tyrant. He was a God of incredible love, whose heart longed for lost sheep, lost coins, and lost boys to be found. He was not the God of the medieval church that was greatly feared, but rather He is a God of overwhelming love to be worshiped. The Scriptures revealed a God far beyond Huss's imagination. English scholar and theologian C. S. Lewis, in describing his own conversion from atheism to theism and then to Christianity, describes God this way: "The hardness of God is kinder than the softness of men, and His compulsion is our liberation."[3]

For Huss and tens of thousands in Europe, this view of God was revolutionary. No longer were they held captive to fear. They, too, were "surprised by joy" and could rejoice in a God who loved them more than they could possibly imagine. They discovered Christ who came to "proclaim liberty to the captives and . . . set at liberty those who are oppressed" (Luke 4:18, 19; Isaiah 61:1, 2). The Holy Spirit speaking through the words of Scripture became the foundation of Huss's and his followers' faith. God's Word became their guide. His love became the motivating factor in their lives. Christ's grace and goodness became the essence of their glorious song.

For the first time in their lives their worship became a joyous celebration of their faith in the Christ who redeemed them. Tradition and church dogma lost its hold upon them. The excesses of the medieval priests and their abuse of power were a stark contrast to the simplicity and humility that they discovered in the Christ of Scripture. John Huss did not hesitate to fearlessly share his findings with his congregation at the Bethlehem Chapel. Week after week, he proclaimed the unadulterated truth of God's Word. He unashamedly and powerfully proclaimed the greatness of God, the supremacy of the Scriptures, and the free grace of Christ. He unapologetically exposed the abuses and errors of the medieval church.

Truth opposed but triumphant

Huss's preaching led to violent opposition from the Roman Church. Eventually he was summoned to Constance and, like his Master, unjustly tried and wrongfully condemned. Although he had been given a safe conduct of protection by Sigismund, King of the Romans and leader of the Holy Roman Empire, the prelates of the church persuaded the king to violate his word and imprison John Huss during his trial. The conditions in the prison were abominable. The dark, damp dungeon chilled Huss's feeble body. The harsh conditions weakened his already weary frame, and he developed a fever that nearly ended his life. Finally he was brought before the council for his trial. "Loaded with chains he stood in the presence of the emperor, whose honor and good faith had been pledged to protect him. During his long trial he firmly maintained the truth, and in the presence of the assembled dignitaries of church and state he uttered a solemn and faithful protest against the corruptions of the hierarchy. When required to choose whether he would recant his doctrines or suffer death, he accepted the martyr's fate."[4]

Miraculously, God sustained Huss in his time of deepest trial. His life work was not yet completed. He would bear witness to the truth before the leading princes and prelates of the day. The truth would echo boldly through the chambers of the emperor's court and echo from those halls to the ends of the earth.

James Russell Lowell stated it well:

"Once to every man and nation comes the moment
    to decide,
In the strife of Truth with Falsehood, for the good
    or evil side; . . .
Truth forever on the scaffold, Wrong forever on the
    throne,—
Yet that scaffold sways the future, and, behind the
    dim unknown,
Standeth God within the shadow, keeping watch,
    above his own."[5]

John Huss's commitment was firm. His decision was unwavering. Like the prophet Daniel two millennia earlier, he "purposed in his heart" to serve God and could not be moved (Daniel 1:8). Huss knew that although the king could sentence him to death, he could not destroy the truth of God's Word.

As Jesus said, "Heaven and earth will pass away, but

my words will by no means pass away" (Matthew 24:35). The apostle Paul added, "For we can do nothing against the truth, but for the truth" (2 Corinthians 13:8). God's truth will triumph at last. In the face of the fiercest persecution, the truth of God will one day lighten the earth with the glory of God (see Revelation 18:1). The darkness that enshrouds the mind about the true character of God and His changeless love will fade into obscurity in the light of His eternal truth. Those who stand with Christ for the truth of His Word will triumph with the truth.

Heaven's peace

In spite of the intense suffering he experienced for weeks before his trial, Huss was at peace. Visitors to his lowly cell noted his unusual serenity. Heaven's peace filled his soul. " 'I write this letter,' he said to a friend, 'in my prison, and with my fettered hand, expecting my sentence of death tomorrow. . . . When, with the assistance of Jesus Christ, we shall again meet in the delicious peace of the future life, you will learn how merciful God has shown Himself toward me, how effectually He has supported me in the midst of my temptations and trials.' "[6] His was a peace "that passes all understanding" (Philippians 4:7). His inner peace testified to the eternal truth that God is present in our greatest trials and in our times of greatest need.

On July 6, 1415, John Huss was led through the streets of Constance to be burned at the stake. The executioner securely fastened his hands behind him and lashed him to a wooden pole. Huss was placed on top of a pile of dry branches. As the flames were lit and the wooden pile set ablaze, Huss began singing, "Jesus, Son of David, have mercy on me!" Witnesses testified that Huss uttered no cry of pain. He almost seemed to rejoice as if he were going to a wedding. He had lived well, and he could die well.

What gave John Huss and the other martyrs such death-defying faith? What enabled them to face torture, persecution, and death itself? Their Savior had conquered the grave. Jesus was unjustly tried, condemned, and sentenced to die. His death on the cross was the cruelest of all deaths imaginable. Yet hanging on the cross He prayed, "Father forgive them, for they know not what they do." Although the disciples faced the darkest of Fridays, they also experienced the most amazing of all Sundays. There was joy in the morning. Christ rose from the dead that Sunday morning. The darkened grave could not hold Him. The sealed tomb could not shut Him in. Death would not have the last word. The One who is "the resurrection and the life" triumphed over the grave and the powers of hell. Every time Jesus confronted death, He won.

In the light of heaven's glory, the Roman soldiers guarding His tomb fell over as dead men. The angel rolled away the huge gravestone sealing the tomb as a pebble. Heaven announced before the entire universe, "Son, thy Father calleth thee," and Jesus came out of the grave alive. Death was a defeated foe. Christ conquered the tomb, and forever after His faithful followers would have hope. Down through the centuries, faithful Christian believers could face the fiercest persecutions, unimaginable sufferings, and torturous deaths because they had the undeniable assurance that Christ had conquered death and promised to be with them even "to the end of the world."

John Huss grasped this hope and died believing that although his body was burned in the flames, the truth he lived and died for would ultimately triumph. When his body had been totally consumed, his ashes were collected and cast into the Rhine River. His enemies believed that even the memory of Huss would soon be forgotten and the truths he stood for would be obliterated forever. They thought that once and for all, the Bible teachings he stood for would be wiped off the face of the earth. Although his voice was silenced in death, the influence of his life still speaks through the ages. The apostle John stated this eternal truth in the Bible's closing book, Revelation: " 'Blessed are the dead that die in the Lord from now on.' 'Yes,' says the Spirit, 'that they may rest from their labors, and their works follow them' " (Revelation 14:13).

> Little did they [his persecutors] dream that the ashes that day borne away to the sea were to be as seed scattered in all the countries of the earth; that in lands yet unknown it would yield abundant fruit in witnesses for the truth. The voice which had spoken in the council hall of Constance had wakened echoes that would be heard through all coming ages. Huss was no more, but the truths for which he died could never perish. His example of faith and constancy would encourage multitudes

to stand firm for the truth, in the face of torture and death.[7]

Truth cannot be burned. It cannot be destroyed. It cannot be blotted out. It cannot be obliterated. The wonderful, incredible, amazing good news is that truth will triumph at last. Jesus will win. Satan will lose, and one day truth will echo throughout the universe.

1. White, *The Great Controversy*, 102.

2. J. F. X. O'Conor, *A Study of Francis Thompson's Hound of Heaven*, 4th ed. (New York: John Lane Company, 1912), 7.

3. C. S. Lewis, *Surprised by Joy*, reissue ed. (New York: HarperOne, 2017), 280.

4. White, *The Great Controversy*, 107.

5. James Russell Lowell, "The Present Crisis," in *The Poetical Works of James Russell Lowell* (Cambridge, MA: Riverside Press, 1904), 68.

6. White, *The Great Controversy*, 107.

7. Ibid., 110.

Chapter 4

Amazed by Grace

God is not impressed with wealth; He owns the world. He is not impressed with power; He created the planets. He is not impressed with position; He rules the universe. And one day He will come as King of kings and Lord of lords. What God is impressed with is character. When an individual commits their life to Christ and, through His grace, determines to live a godly life, God notices.

Martin Luther was raised in the humble home of a German peasant in the midst of poverty, privation, and hardship. His father was a miner, and although he was a diligent worker, times were hard and life was tough for his family. When Martin went to school, he often had to sing from door to door to get enough money to buy a few morsels of food. Think of how embarrassing this was for a young teenage boy who had no other choice—if he wanted to eat. God was preparing Luther in the school of hardship to endure trials and face difficulties with courage.

God often prepares us for the future by allowing us to face challenges today. It is in the context of these trials that we learn to trust God more deeply. A life of trust is rarely learned through a life of ease. The severity of Luther's school days and the poverty he experienced produced a tenacity in his character that would serve him well in future years. He would need an unshakable faith combined with an unflinching courage to challenge the abuses of the medieval church.

Martin Luther had an unusually brilliant mind. He enrolled in the University of Erfurt at eighteen to become a priest. This greatly upset and displeased his father. Luther's father recognized the abuses in the church and wanted his son to become a lawyer. Martin soon distinguished himself as one of the university's brightest scholars. His sharp intellectual skills united with his resolute character and disciplined study habits catapulted him to the top of his class. But there was one thing that stood out in Luther's life that set him apart even more than his academic excellence—his sincerity of purpose that characterized his entire life. He had an inner hunger to know God. He longed to live a godly life but was perplexed to understand how to best please God. For years he struggled in fear, doubt, and insecurity.

A turning point

One day while studying in the university library, Luther came to a turning point in his life. He discovered a Latin copy of the Bible. He had heard sections of the Gospels and Paul's epistles preached at church but never held a copy of the entire Bible in his hands. With sheer delight, he read chapter after chapter, verse after verse. He was amazed at the clarity and power of God's Word. Its undiluted truth, in contrast with the stale traditions of the church, overwhelmed him. Describing his first experience with the Bible, he wrote, "Oh! that God would give me such a book for myself!" Luther spent every spare moment studying the Scriptures. He had a new love—the Word of God. Its charm and attraction won his heart and drew him back to its pages again and again.

As he continued to study the Bible, he developed a sense of God's holiness and his own unworthiness. He longed to live a godly, righteous life but felt weak and incapable of meeting God's righteous standards. His own inadequacy and human frailty discouraged him greatly. The more he considered his sinfulness, the more discouraged he became. It appeared there was nothing he could do to meet God's righteous demands. He fasted. He practiced self-denial. He flagellated his body. He prayed and prayed some more, but somehow he just could not seem to please God with all of his monkish works.

When Luther was at the point of physical, mental, emotional, and spiritual exhaustion, God brought an older priest into his life who became a godly mentor. This pious man, John Staupitz, counseled Luther to look away from himself to Jesus. He urged him to "trust in the righteousness of Christ's life" and to believe that grace flowed through the cross to forgive his sins, pardon his guilt, and make full, complete atonement for his unrighteousness. Staupitz shared the meaning of grace with Luther, and for the first time in his life Luther began to grasp the divine reality that although he was a great sinner, Jesus was a great Savior. Although his sins were many, God's grace was enough, more than enough, to pardon them all and enable him to live a righteous life. For the first time, peace flooded his soul. Joy filled his heart. The grace of God was enough to meet the righteous demands of the law. A new day was dawning. The light of God's grace, the majesty of His love, and a revelation of His goodness penetrated the darkness of Luther's discouraged soul, and he was never the same again.

Changed by grace

Luther was ordained as a priest and appointed to the church at Wittenberg. It was there that he began to preach with power the message of God's grace and Christ's righteousness week after week. Crowds flocked to hear his heartfelt, life-changing messages. His words were like a draft of cold water in the barren desert of their lives. They were shackled by the traditions of the medieval church and kept in bondage with centuries-old rituals that provided no spiritual life. Luther's biblical messages made a difference. They touched hearts, and lives were changed. What was this message that Luther preached? Why was it so powerful to change lives?

As Luther read the New Testament, he was overwhelmed with the goodness of God. He was amazed at God's loving desire to save all mankind. The popular view taught by church leaders at the time was that salvation was partly a human work and partly God's work. Luther believed, and rightly so, that salvation was totally and completely the work of God that believers receive by faith. He rejoiced in passages like this: "For by grace you have been saved through faith, and that not of yourselves; it is the gift of God, not of works, lest anyone should boast. For we are His workmanship, created in Christ Jesus for good works, which God prepared beforehand that we should walk in them" (Ephesians 2:8–10).

God has provided salvation as a gift. His Holy Spirit leads us to accept by faith what Christ has so freely provided through His death on Calvary's cross. There on the cross, Jesus, the divine Son of God, offered His perfect life to atone for our sinfulness. Divine justice demands perfect obedience, and the divine law we have broken condemns us to eternal death. The Bible is clear. "All have sinned and fall short of the glory of God" (Romans 3:23). Through our sinful choices we have "fallen short" of God's ideal for our lives. We have sinned. We have rebelled against God. Left to ourselves, we cannot meet the just, righteous demands of a holy God. As a result, we deserve eternal death. But there is good news. Christ's perfect life stands in the place of our imperfect lives. The apostle Paul assures us, "The wages of sin is death, but the gift of God is eternal life in Christ Jesus our Lord" (Romans 6:23). The book *The Desire of Ages* puts it this way: "Christ was treated as we deserve, that we might be treated as He deserves. He was condemned for our sins, in which He had no share, that we might be justified by His righteousness, in which we had no share. He suffered the death which was ours, that we might receive the life which was His."[1]

Martin Luther explained his understanding of righteousness by faith in a series of statements titled the Smalcald Articles. There he stated,

. . . The first and chief article.

1] That Jesus Christ, our God and Lord, died for our sins, and was raised again for our justification, Rom. 4:25.

2] And He alone is the Lamb of God which taketh away the sins of the world, John 1:29; and God has laid on Him the iniquity of us all, Is. 53:6.

3] Likewise: All have sinned and are justified without merit [freely, and without their own works or merits] by His grace, through the redemption that is in Christ Jesus, in His blood, Rom. 3:23f.

4] Now, since it is necessary to believe this, and it cannot be otherwise acquired or apprehended by any work, law, or merit, it is clear and certain that this faith alone justifies us. . . .

5] Of this article nothing can be yielded or surrendered . . . , even though heaven and earth . . . should sink to ruin.[2]

A new wind was blowing through the Christian church. Tens of thousands of people were taught to look away from their sinful selves and toward Jesus. They were taught to look away from priests and prelates, from traditions and rituals, from church dogma and traditions to Jesus Christ Himself. In Him they found a precious Savior who loved them, died for them, was resurrected from the dead for them, and who desired to save them more than they could ever imagine.

A crisis breaks

Thousands rejoiced in the newfound salvation that

Christ freely offers. Joy flooded their souls. Their hearts were at peace. But a crisis loomed on the horizon. At this time St. Peter's Basilica was being rebuilt in Rome. The pope authorized the selling of indulgences as pardons for sin. Johann Tetzel was the official appointed by the church to lead out in the sale of these indulgences. As he approached a city, a messenger went before him with pomp and pageantry, announcing his arrival. Tetzel declared that the purchase of these indulgences would atone for the sins that a person had committed in the past or would even commit in the future.

Worse yet, he described the loved ones of those present who were burning in purgatory and crying out for deliverance. The poor peasants were heartbroken by the thought of their dead relatives suffering in the flames. When Tetzel had worked up their emotions to a frightful frenzy, he then declared that the indulgences had the power to not only save the living but also deliver the dead from their terrible torment. He appealed to people's deepest emotions when he said that at the sound of their coins dropping into his money chest, the soul of their loved one would be delivered from purgatory. Of course, this was total fabrication and a complete perversion of the Scripture.

Luther sets the record straight

When these peasants came to their pastor with the so-called pardons, Luther decisively pointed out that these indulgences had no standing with God at all. The Scripture says, "When we confess our sins, He [Jesus] is faithful and just to forgive our sins" (1 John 1:9). We receive God's pardon for sin when we confess the sin in sincere repentance before God. Luther refused to recognize Tetzel's indulgences as biblical and declared that the grace of God cannot be purchased. It is a free gift. He urged his parishioners not to purchase these indulgences any longer.

Sensing an urgency to underline his opposition to indulgences in a more forceful and public way, Luther decided to write out clear scriptural reasons why indulgences were unscriptural. All Saints' Day was approaching, and thousands of pilgrims were approaching Wittenberg to give adoration to the many relics that were housed in the church. Luther decided to use this occasion to nail his Ninety-Five Theses against indulgences to the door of the Castle Church in Wittenberg. Hundreds read them. His propositions attracted attention throughout Europe. They were copied and recopied and circulated widely. The sale of indulgences plummeted.

Luther fearlessly preached the word of God. Two pillars of truth supported his teachings: The Bible and the Bible only as a rule of faith and practice; and Christ as the only source of salvation. His teachings cast doubt on the absolute authority of the Church of Rome. He placed Scripture above the traditions of the church and emphasized that Christ was the only true head of the church. Luther was convinced that if the Bible were approached prayerfully, with a sincere desire to do God's will, the Holy Spirit would be the divine interpreter of Scripture, making truth plain to the reader. Jesus confirmed this understanding when He declared, "When He, the Spirit of truth, has come, He will guide you into all truth"

(John 16:13). Jesus also adds, "If anyone wills to do His will, he shall know concerning the doctrine" (John 7:17).

In other words, when we come to Scripture with sincere hearts, seeking to know God and desiring to do His will, the Holy Spirit will reveal truth to us. The Bible is not the exclusive property of a few educated theologians. It reveals God's will for all of us and can be understood by the average person. God speaks through His Word as we approach it with open minds and sincere hearts.

The Word and revival

Spiritual revival broke out all through Europe. The message of the Scriptures touched hearts. In cottages, convents, and castles, the Word of God nourished famished souls. It moved kings, queens, shopkeepers, peasants, and university students. It met with great favor but also great opposition. The psalmist David declares, "Your Word has given me life" (Psalm 119:50).

The Word of God is life giving. It wakes us from spiritual slumber. It renews and enlivens our spiritual lives. When we open the pages of Scripture with the sincere desire to know God, the Holy Spirit not only reveals divine truth but also ministers to us through the Bible to transform our lives.

Tried but faithful

The chorus of voices railing against Luther grew until he was charged with heresy and summoned to Rome to face a trial. He was declared a troublesome heretic and accused of high treason against the church, and his teachings were condemned. Some of his influential friends protested against his going to Rome, fearing that the possibility of his getting a fair trial would be significantly less and his life would be unjustly snuffed out. Their efforts were productive, and the trial was moved to Augsburg in Germany.

Luther journeyed to Augsburg with no fear for his life. His life was committed to Christ, and he did not fear what any human being could do to him. He had already died to his own will and surrendered it to the greater will of his Master. The death of his body was of little matter, because he had the assurance of eternal life in Christ our Lord. He also knew that God's truth would triumph in the end. He had the confidence that no earthly power could stop the progress of God's Word, and he clung to Jesus' assurance to us: "Heaven and earth will pass away, but My words will by no means pass away" (Matthew 24:35).

Throughout his life Luther was criticized and condemned. His writings were banned and burned. He was accused of treason and treachery. His followers were excommunicated from the church. Entire cities that accepted the teachings of Luther were considered to be under the curse of God. His followers were hunted, persecuted, and often martyred. Through all of these trials and in the midst of these challenges, Luther stood firm. His courage did not waver. He had one simple, straightforward message for His accusers: "I am bound by the Scriptures I have quoted, and my conscience is captive to the Word of God. I cannot and will not retract anything, since it is neither safe nor right to go against conscience. May God help me. Amen."

Luther was a man of conviction. He would not sacrifice his conscience to popular opinion. The approval of Christ was more important to him than the approval of any human being or religious leader. He followed the counsel of Solomon, who urged, "Buy the truth, and do not sell it" (Proverbs 23:23).

In an age of moral compromise, when many people face the ethical dilemma of yielding their conscientious convictions to be politically correct, the Holy Spirit speaks in trumpet tones through God's Word: "Buy the truth, and sell it not." To compromise our integrity for popularity or human approval is to sell our souls cheap. The call of the crowd is most often the call to compromise the inner leadings of the Holy Spirit in our lives. We are true to ourselves and our inmost beings when we choose to live by heaven's eternal principles. Our only safety is accepting God's Word and following it wherever it leads.

Luther's enduring legacy

Luther published his German translation of the New Testament in 1522. The translation of the Old Testament was completed in 1534. For the first time, the German nation had the entire Bible in a readable form in their mother tongue. Luther diligently worked to make his new German translation understandable to the average person. He was convinced that the Bible was not the sole possession of scholars. For Luther, it was God's living Word for all mankind.

Luther's translation used a common form of German that was easily understandable for both northern and southern Germans. He claimed, "We are removing impediments and difficulties so that other people may read it without hindrance."[3] It was his dream that the average person would be able to take the Scriptures in their hands and understand the Bible for themselves.

The Bible was the foundation of all Luther's teaching. Christ was the center of his message, and salvation through faith alone was at the core of his preaching.

Luther's call for obedience

Although Luther believed that salvation was through Christ alone, by grace alone, received by faith alone, he did not downplay the need for obedience. He affirmed that the Ten Commandments clearly reveal the will of God and forcefully express how a Christian ought to live. Obedience is the fruit of faith. Jesus stated it clearly when He said, "If you love Me, keep My commandments" (John 14:15). After discussing salvation by grace alone in Romans 3, the apostle Paul adds, "Do we then make void the law through faith? Certainly not! On the contrary, we establish the law" (Romans 3:31). He makes his argument even stronger in Romans 6:15 when he emphatically states, "What then? Shall we sin because we are not under the law but under grace? Certainly not!" Grace does not free us from keeping God's law. It provides both the motivation and the power for obedience.

The call of the Reformation is a call that echoes through the centuries and speaks to those of us living in the twenty-first century. It is a call to faithfulness to the Bible in an age of compromise. It is an appeal that salvation is found in Christ and Christ alone. The message of the Reformation leads us from the self-centeredness of our own lives to total trust in Jesus as the Author of our salvation, grace as the means of salvation, and faith as the hand that grasps the gift of salvation. Saved by grace, we are empowered to live godly, obedient lives. Rejoicing in the gift of His salvation, living in the power of His grace, we long to obey Him. Christ is both our Savior and our Lord.

Amazed by His grace, charmed by His love, and enthralled by His goodness, we desire nothing else than to serve Him forever. We can do no less for the one who has done so much for us. Duty becomes a delight, and sacrifice becomes a pleasure. Our obedience is the response to the gift of salvation He so freely offers. Our greatest joy is bringing joy to the heart of the One who has paid such an infinite cost for our salvation. He gave so much and, in comparison, requires so little that all we can do is find our greatest joy in obeying Him. I invite you to enter into the joy of His salvation. He freely offers it to you right now. Will you receive it? Accept the fact that He has died to redeem you. Believe that the gift of salvation is yours by faith. Open your heart to receive the wonders of His grace. Enter into the joy of living for Jesus and serving Him today and forever.

1. Ellen G. White, *The Desire of Ages*, 25.

2. Martin Luther, "The Smalcald Articles," *The Book of Concord: The Confessions of the Lutheran Church*, http://bookofconcord.org/smalcald.php#officeandworkofjesus.

3. Derek Wilson, *Out of the Storm* (New York: St. Martin's, 2007), 302.

Truth Seekers

Throughout the centuries, men and women have earnestly sought for the truth about the great questions of life. They have pondered questions like, *What is the meaning of life? How can I find inner peace? Where can I find hope for the future? Why is there so much suffering in the world? Is there a God and does He care for me? Is there a divine, infallible source of truth that provides the answers to life's deepest questions?* Tens of thousands of people have discovered meaningful answers to these questions in the Bible. The Scriptures provided them with the key to unlock the mysteries of life. The Word of God became a solid foundation to face life's challenges.

In the Middle Ages, from the fifth to the fifteenth centuries, when the light of truth was obscured by the darkness of superstition and tradition, humble men and women of God sought earnestly for truth. They longed for the peace that only Christ can give. Their hearts yearned for a genuine, authentic experience with God. They were tired of the pretense and hypocrisy of a religion that focused on externals but left the soul barren. The intense search to discover real spirituality in the outer ornaments of religion through their own human efforts left them spiritually exhausted. They wanted more, much more than some superficial, artificial religiosity.

What was it that motivated these truth seekers in the Middle Ages? They longed to know God. They had a heart hunger for the eternal truths of His word. The Old Testament prophet Jeremiah puts it this way: "You will seek Me and find Me, when you search for Me with all your heart" (Jeremiah 29:13). The psalmist David adds, "As the deer pants for the water brooks, so pants my soul for you, O God. My soul thirsts for God, for the living God" (Psalm 42:1, 2). There is one common thread that runs through the lives of the great Reformers: they had a longing to know God.

They came from different backgrounds. Many of them were highly educated, but some were not. Some were born into wealthy families. Others were born into poor homes. Some were brought up among the teeming masses of the cities. Others were raised in the obscurity of country villages. They came from the various countries in Europe and spoke different languages. But whatever their background, they had an unquenchable desire to know God. This is the longing of all humanity. As Augustine put it so well, "You have made us for yourself, and our heart is restless until it rests in you."[1]

The universal testimony of these men and women of God in the Middle Ages is as true in the twenty-first century as it was centuries ago. Once again, in this generation, in the glitz and glamour of a technological, media-savvy age that bombards us with ten thousand messages a day on social media, there is a heart hunger for authentic relationships. A daily tweet or an instant message does not satisfy the longing of the soul for the eternal. It does not fill the aching void in the heart for a genuine relationship with God.

Lessons from the past

Someone has said we are doomed to repeat history if we do not learn its lessons. What lessons can we discover about knowing God in the lives of these faithful spiritual giants of the past? What can they teach us about going deeper in our own spiritual experience? What lessons leap off the pages of history about knowing truth and the cost of following it? In this chapter we will review the lives of some of these reformers and discover vital steps on the pathway of knowing God. As we take this journey together we will explore just how these spiritual giants, with all of their human weakness, experienced the presence of God, discovered the truth of God, and walked in the ways of God.

We begin our journey in France. Long before the Reformation began in Germany, the dawn of a new day began in France. A professor at the University of Paris began to study ancient literature, and his attention was directed to the Bible. Lefevre had never studied the Bible before. It was a new book to him. He hadn't given it much thought previously, but as he carefully studied its pages something remarkable happened in his life. He was strangely drawn to the Christ of Scripture. His heart was touched. His soul was warmed. A new sense of peace flooded his life. The thought that God loved him and sent His Son to bear the guilt and condemnation of his sins overwhelmed him. He discovered the reality that he was a lost sinner condemned to eternal death without Christ, but through the acceptance of Jesus' perfect life and sacrifice on the cross he would have eternal life.

Overwhelmed with joy, he wrote, "Oh! The unspeakable greatness of that exchange,—the Sinless One is condemned, and he who is guilty goes free,—the Blessing bears the curse, and the cursed is brought into blessing,—the Life dies, and the dead live,—the Glory is whelmed in darkness, and he who knew nothing but confusion of face is clothed with glory."[2]

Here is a common characteristic of the Reformers and all truth seekers. They become disillusioned with their own spiritual experience and begin an intense search for something more. The Holy Spirit leads them to the Word of God. In the Bible they discover the living Christ, and their lives are changed. In Him they find their hearts' desire.

One of Lefevre's students, William Farel, had a similar experience. The son of godly parents, he was a devoted follower of the teachings of the medieval church. He made the rounds of the churches in Paris, worshiping at their altars and bringing offerings to their shrines, but he could not find peace. The nagging guilt of his unworthiness and a sense of condemnation before God left his soul barren. Conviction of sin tormented him. If only he could find peace!

Farel was an earnest seeker after truth. While listening to Lefevre's words he was impressed with this thought:

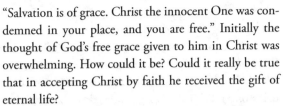

"Salvation is of grace. Christ the innocent One was condemned in your place, and you are free." Initially the thought of God's free grace given to him in Christ was overwhelming. How could it be? Could it really be true that in accepting Christ by faith he received the gift of eternal life?

Let's pause for a moment and see if we too can discover this amazing grace of our Lord Jesus Christ. Let's see if we can find the eternal truths of God's Word regarding salvation as they discovered them centuries ago. These life-changing truths transformed their lives, and they can transform ours too.

Salvation's story

What was it that these seekers after truth found in the Scriptures that changed their lives? The books of Romans and Ephesians were particularly precious to them. In Romans they discovered the eternal truth that in their own hearts they knew to be all too true: "All have sinned and fall short of the glory of God" (Romans 3:23). Deep within the fabric of our beings, we sense it too. We have sinned. We have fallen short of God's ideal for our lives. They trembled at the thought that the "wages of sin is death" (Romans 6:23). Even their good works were, at times, prompted by selfish motives. They seemed bound in chains of self-centeredness, pride, greed, and lust. At times, uncontrollable passions burst forth like a mighty torrent. Like a helpless prisoner in the loneliness of a prison cell, they longed for deliverance, and they found the answer in Scripture.

The Bible not only presents the problem but also

offers the solution. Although all have sinned and come short of the glory of God, we are "justified freely by His grace through the redemption that is in Christ Jesus" (Romans 3:24). Yes, the wages of sin is death, but "the gift of God is eternal life in Jesus Christ our Lord" (Romans 6:23). Salvation is a gift offered freely by God to all who accept it by faith. To men and women vainly struggling to secure their salvation by good works and who never seemed to be good enough, this was incredible good news. To people desperate for a ray of hope, the free grace of God was a thought almost too good to be true.

When they read Ephesians 2:8–10, their hearts leapt for joy. "For by grace you have been saved through faith, and that not of yourselves; it is the gift of God, not of works, lest anyone should boast. For we are His workmanship, created in Christ Jesus for good works, which God prepared beforehand that we should walk in them." Salvation is always through Christ. When I look at myself with all my imperfections, faults, and weaknesses, it appears that it is impossible for me to be saved. When I look at Jesus in all of His righteousness and perfection, it appears that it is impossible for me to be lost.

Accepting Christ means that by faith I receive the righteousness of His life in the place of my unrighteousness, that I accept His death on the cross in the place of my eternal death, and that I accept the reality of the fact that through His Holy Spirit He lives in me to make me the person I long to be. The apostle John puts it this way: "And this is the testimony: that God has given us eternal life, and this life is in His Son. He who has the Son has l:ᶠ ᴧe who does not have the Son of God does not have ᴧre. These things I have written to you who believe in the name of the Son of God, that you may know that you have eternal life, and that you may continue to believe in the name of the Son of God" (1 John 5:11–13).

Belief: An act of the will

Belief is an act of the will. Prompted by the Holy Spirit, we choose to believe. It is that simple. Salvation is not complicated. Accepting Jesus is a choice. As I recognize that I have sinned and fallen short of the divine ideal, I must grasp the fact that He loves me and He made the ultimate sacrifice to save me, and I must acknowledge that my sins have broken His heart. I repent, confess my sin, and believe I am forgiven. In accepting the eternal life He freely offers, I live a new life empowered by His Spirit. The apostle Paul puts it this way: "Therefore, if anyone is in Christ, he is a new creation; old things have passed away; behold, all things have become new" (2 Corinthians 5:17).

When the light of the truth of salvation dawned upon the hearts of these Reformers, it changed their lives. They were filled up with God's love. Their lives overflowed with God's grace. And as the apostle Paul so aptly put it, "I am not ashamed of the gospel of Christ, for it is the power of God to salvation for everyone who believes, for the Jew first and also for the Greek" (Romans 1:16). The salvation Christ so freely provided was for all peoples everywhere. Changed by the grace of God, these men and women of faith were compelled to tell the story.

Lefevre worked diligently to translate the New

Testament into the French language. All of France must be able to read the story of salvation for themselves. Farel returned to his native town in eastern France and passionately proclaimed the good news of Jesus. When the authorities drove him out of the major cities, he traversed the plains and villages, preaching God's Word in private dwellings, in quiet villages, and in secluded mountain valleys. He kept moving from place to place to avoid the persecution of the state-church authorities. He often slept in the forests or in the rocky crevices of some mountain pass. Although fiercely persecuted, he continued preaching the message of salvation by faith in Jesus' grace alone.

God's Spirit moved upon the hearts of men and women throughout Europe. He was raising up a generation that would change the history of the world. The "good news" of Christ's grace that they discovered was so good, they had to share it. No amount of slander, ridicule, or persecution could silence their voices.

John Calvin was a brilliant young priest who struggled to find salvation's peace. One day he witnessed the burning of a so-called heretic in a public square. He was incredibly moved by the look of peace on this man's face. Amid torture and a dreadful death, this martyr exhibited a faith and courage that deeply impressed the young John Calvin.

Calvin knew that this "heretic" based his faith on the teachings of Scripture. He determined to study the Bible until he grasped the reason for this man's undaunted faith. As Calvin pored over the teachings of Scripture, he discovered a Christ more marvelous than his fondest dreams. With joy he exclaimed, "His blood has washed away my impurities; his cross has borne my curse; His death has atoned for me."[3] The gospel of Christ so deeply moved John Calvin that he gave his entire life to preaching the joys of salvation. He was able to endure suffering, experience ridicule, face persecution, and toil in poverty for the sake of the gospel.

Calvin powerfully proclaimed the free grace of Christ throughout France. While in Paris, as he was preparing to spend time in quiet meditation, thoughtful Bible study, and earnest prayer, he heard from friends that the authorities were preparing to take his life. A martyr's death at the flames awaited him. Some of his friends detained the authorities at the door while he was let down from a window and escaped. He was led by friends to the home of a poor farmer, disguised as a peasant, and with a hoe over his shoulder, he cautiously made his way to safety.

Terrible persecution bloodied the streets of France. Thousands were tortured and brutally slaughtered—their only crime their belief in the truths of the Bible. Eventually Calvin settled in Geneva, and for nearly thirty years he labored there to advance the cause of Christ. Calvin did not understand truth perfectly. His understanding of religious freedom was certainly limited; nevertheless, he was unmoved in his commitment to Scripture, his devotion to Christ, and his unwavering desire to share the Christ he loved with others.

The light penetrates the darkness

Each one of these Reformers grasped a portion of God's truth. They did not comprehend the fullness of truth.

Their comprehension was limited. God was leading them out of the darkness of superstition and error. The fullness of Bible truth had been hidden under the rubbish of error for centuries. The wise man said, "The path of the just is like the shining sun, that shines ever brighter unto the perfect day" (Proverbs 4:18). When the sun rises in the morning, initially it is not very light. As the day dawns, the light gradually chases away the darkness.

Have you ever left a dark room and walked directly into the sunlight? What happens when this occurs? You are blinded by the light. Light is good, but too much too quickly can blind you. The sun rises gradually, gladdening the earth with its warming rays.

The wise man says, that is what understanding God's truth is like. God does not throw a cosmic switch and illuminate the earth all at once with the brightness of the sun. The sun rises slowly, chasing away the darkness. Similarly, the light of God's truth rose slowly in the hearts and minds of His people over the centuries. No one person grasped the fullness of God's truth. Each one contributed to the whole. As they studied the Scriptures, men and women of God made contributions to understanding His divine plan.

Although they were different in their understanding of some things, each of these Reformers of the Middle Ages were totally committed to diligently studying the Word of God, discovering the will of God, accepting the gift of salvation freely given by God, and living a life of obedience to God. They rejected the idea that the decrees of the church hierarchy were a higher authority than the authority of the Bible. They could not conscientiously accept the notion that the traditions of the church were more important than the doctrines of Christ. To these faithful people of God, if truth was worth dying for, it was certainly worth living for. They could testify with the apostle Paul, as he so eloquently spoke from a Roman prison, "For to me, to live is Christ, but to die is gain" (Philippians 1:21).

They had experienced the joy of salvation. The hope of eternal life burned brightly in their hearts. Nothing in this world could rob them of the peace they enjoyed in Christ. The more they discovered about Jesus in His Word, the more they loved Him. The more they understood about His unselfish character of divine love, the more they wanted to learn. The more they knew of His grace, the more they wanted to experience.

These men and woman of faith were unafraid to share their testimony of God's goodness and grace with others. The gospel of His grace could not be left unshared and bottled up in their hearts. Christ and Christ alone satisfied their inner longing. Christ and Christ alone met the needs of their heart. Christ and Christ alone was the Source of their peace and joy. Christ and Christ alone delivered them from guilt, forgave their sins, and gave them new hope.

When the odds were stacked against them, their faith was unshakable. When they experienced peril and persecution, trials and torture, poverty and perplexity, they rejoiced to be counted worthy to share with Christ in His sufferings (1 Peter 1:21). Writing to the Corinthian church, the apostle Paul exclaims, "But of Him you are in Christ Jesus, who became for us wisdom from God— and righteousness and sanctification and redemption" (1 Corinthians 1:30).

You and I can experience His grace as well. It is ours for the asking. He is our righteousness. He is our peace. He is the source of our salvation. He is the river of our joy. In Christ we are complete. In Christ we are forgiven. In Christ we are redeemed. In Christ we are a "new creation." Reach out for life today, and accept all that Christ offers you right now!

---

1. *Augustine's Confessions*, ed. Leland Ryken (Wheaton, IL: Crossway, 2015).

2. J. H. Merle-D'Aubigné, *History of the Great Reformation of the Sixteenth Century in Germany, Switzerland, Etc.* (Philadelphia: Porter and Coates, 1870), bk.12, 379.

3. J. H. Merle-D'Aubigné, *History of the Reformation in Europe in the Time of Calvin* (New York: Carter and Brothers, 1867), bk. II, 47.

Chapter 6

No Price Too High

When we consider the life of Bible-believing Christians in the Middle Ages, it becomes increasingly obvious that many of them paid an extremely high price for their faith. They were tortured, imprisoned, exiled, and executed. Their properties were confiscated, their homes burned, their lands ravished, and their families persecuted. Yet, like the apostle Paul, they praised God in prison. When they were driven from their homes, they looked for a "city whose builder and maker is God." When they were tortured they blessed their tormentors, and when they languished in dark, damp, dungeons, they claimed God's promises of a brighter tomorrow. Although their bodies were imprisoned, they were free— free in Christ, free in the truths of His Word. His grace set them free. And although locked in prison cells, they were in bondage no longer.

They had discovered the Pearl of great price, and no price was too high to pay for the joy of serving the Christ who had given everything for them. They lived and died for one purpose: to honor Christ and share the truths of His Word with everyone possible. These courageous men and women of faith were willing to pay any price to advance the cause of Christ. Their lives were given to a higher, nobler purpose than living for themselves. Seeing the corruption in the medieval church and recognizing its abuses, they dedicated themselves to placing the Bible in the hands of ordinary people.

A most precious gift

William Tyndale was passionate about giving the English-speaking peoples of the world an accurate, readable translation of the Bible. He was profoundly convinced that without a knowledge of the Scriptures, the average person would never be established in the truths of God's Word. Tyndale was a brilliant scholar who was educated at Oxford and Cambridge universities. He was a gifted linguist, fluent in eight languages—French, Greek, Hebrew, German, Italian, Latin, Spanish, and English. In a heated argument, one of the church leaders of the day tried to convince Tyndale that the teachings and traditions of the church were superior to the teachings of the Word of God. The pompous prelate argued that the average person could not understand Scripture. Tyndale responded, "If God spare my life, ere many yeares I wyl cause a boy that driveth the plough to know more of the Scripture, than [thou] doust."[1]

True to his word, Tyndale began the translation of the Scriptures into English. He was vehemently opposed in England, so he traveled to the European continent to continue and eventually complete his work of translation. Initially, he found a refuge in Luther's Germany, but in a short time he faced fierce opposition again. Twice his work was stopped, but he did not give up. God had placed a dream in his heart, and he would not cease until his work of Bible translation was completed. He had confidence that God would find a way for him to complete his work.

On one occasion, a large shipment of Bibles was secretly shipped to England. At this time the British ports were carefully guarded in an attempt to discover any contraband materials—including English Bibles. Tyndale was shipping the Bibles to a friend who was a bookseller. Soon after its arrival, the entire shipment of Bibles was purchased by the Bishop of Durham with the purpose of destroying them. He thought that this would greatly hinder Tyndale's work. But God was at work in mysterious ways. The bishop's money was used to purchase more paper for better-quality Bibles and aided in furthering the cause of truth rather than hindering it. Later, when Tyndale was tried for his faith, he was asked for the names of those who supported his work. He was promised his freedom if he would divulge the names of those who supported him and provided the funds for his work to go forward. Tyndale declared that the one who helped him more than anyone else was the Bishop of Durham.

Facing his own bout with opposition, the apostle Paul confidently stated an eternal truth: "We can do nothing against the truth, but for the truth" (2 Corinthians 13:8). All of the enemy's efforts to completely stop or destroy Tyndale's work failed. In 1525 he found safe haven in Worms—the city where Luther was tried. There he completed the work of translating the New Testament into English in 1526.

Tyndale was declared a heretic. Many of the Bibles printed in Worms were seized and publicly burned. In 1536 Tyndale was tried on the charge of heresy and condemned to be burned at the stake. He was strangled to death while tied to the stake, then burned. His dying words were spoken with zeal in a loud voice and were reported as, "Lord, open the King of England's eyes." God miraculously answered Tyndale's prayer. Within four years, four English translations of the Bible were published. Later, in 1611, the King James Version of the Bible was published, and it was largely based on Tyndale's work. The fifty-four scholars who produced the work drew heavily from Tyndale's previous English translation. One estimate suggests that the Old Testament of the King James Version is 76 percent Tyndale's translation, and the New Testament is 83 percent. In 2011 the King James Version of the Bible celebrated its four-hundredth anniversary by passing the milestone of one billion Bibles in print. Translated at least partly into 3,223 languages, the Bible has affected tens of millions of people around the globe.[2] William Tyndale's sacrifice was well worth it.

No matter how difficult it seemed or how challenging the circumstances were, Tyndale, along with his Bible-believing Christian colleagues, believed that God was on His throne and He was working all things out according to His will. Although betrayed into the hands of his enemies, imprisoned for months, and finally martyred for his faith, Tyndale produced work that still lives on, and his faithfulness inspires millions today.

Together in commitment

The Holy Spirit moved upon the hearts of men and women throughout England to lead the church back to the Christ of Scripture as the only means of salvation and the Bible as the basis of all true religion. Although revival often begins with one man or one woman, it does not end there. When God initiates spiritual renewal in the heart of a husband, it affects his wife and children. When the Holy Spirit moves upon a wife and mother, it affects her whole family. When God powerfully moves upon the heart of an individual, it often influences neighborhoods and entire communities.

This was certainly the case with Hugh Latimer. Latimer was a brilliant scholar in England who began studying Latin at the age of four. He attended Cambridge University and became a devoted antagonist to the Reformers. He argued vehemently against the teachings of Martin Luther's companion, Philip Melanchthon. Like Saul in the New Testament, he railed against the opposition, condemning them to eternal loss. Each theology graduate at Cambridge had to choose a subject to dispute in his final written exam. Latimer's paper focused on the errors of the new religious ideas taught by the Reformers. He violently opposed any teaching that appeared to undermine the traditions of the medieval church.

Thomas Bilney, a Bible-believing Christian, conceived a plan of how he might influence Latimer. He asked if Latimer would hear his confession. When Latimer agreed, Bilney shared his confession of Christ. He shared the peace and joy that Christ had placed in his heart. He openly spoke about the assurance and security he found in knowing salvation's story. He testified of the change in his life that came in knowing that he was saved through the grace of His Redeemer.

Latimer's heart was deeply moved. He was impressed that Bilney had discovered something that he desperately wanted. There was an aching, a longing in his soul that only Christ could fulfill. As he investigated the claims of Christianity, he, too, was converted to Christ. Once he was converted, Hugh Latimer became a powerful advocate for the truths of the Bible.

Although Tyndale's translation of the Bible had recently been banned, Latimer preached publicly on the importance of people reading the Bible in their own language. He declared that the people ought to read the Bible in their mother tongue and that it contained the might and power of God. Along with the other Reformers, he maintained the absolute authority of the Scriptures.

For more than fifteen years Latimer preached powerful, biblical sermons to hundreds of eager listeners. Their hearts were touched by the grace of God, and their lives were changed through His Word. When he opposed the Articles of Faith based on tradition decreed by Henry VIII, a showdown was inevitable. Latimer was arrested, imprisoned in the Tower of London, and later, along with Nicolas Ridley and Thomas Cranmer, burned at the stake for heresy in Oxford in 1555. When the flames were about to consume them, Latimer encouraged his friend Ridley with these words: "Be of good comfort, Master Ridley, and play the man: we shall this day light such a candle, by God's grace, in England, as I trust shall never be put out."[3]

Although the flames consuming those godly Christian martyrs in the streets of Oxford that day snuffed out their lives, they could not extinguish the truth. The fires of truth, ignited by the Word of God, will illuminate this world with the glory of God. God's truth will triumph at last. God's word, though opposed and oppressed, can never be destroyed. The prophet Isaiah puts it this way: "The grass withers, the flower fades, but the Word of our God stands forever" (Isaiah 40:8). When we accept the teachings of the Bible and choose to live in harmony with the principles of God's Word, we are on the winning side. Truth will triumph at last. Evil will not have the last word; Christ will. The testimony of the faithful martyrs of the past rings with assurance that though truth is cast down, it will rise again in triumph. When one Reformer was martyred, God raised up other—even mightier—men and women of God to carry on the work that they so nobly died for.

Proclaiming advancing light

Each generation experienced more light and truth than the one before it. The wise man says, "The path of the just is like the shining sun, that shines ever brighter unto the perfect day" (Proverbs 4:18). It is not very light at five in the morning. It is lighter at 6:00 A.M., still lighter at 9:00 A.M., and the light of the perfect day fully brightens the sky at noon. God gradually reveals truth so that He will not blind us. Coming out of the darkness of the medieval period, no one person was able to comprehend all of the truth at once. In His infinite wisdom, our Lord revealed truth gradually.

The apostle Paul states this eternal truth in these words: "For we are God's fellow workers; you are God's field, you are God's building. According to the grace of God which was given to me, as a wise master builder I have laid the foundation, and another builds on it. But let each one take heed how he builds on it. For no other foundation can anyone lay than that which is laid, which is Jesus Christ" (1 Corinthians 3:9–11). In every age God reveals more truth to His people. Truth is progressive. There is never a time we can be stagnant in our Christian experience. God is constantly leading us on to understand more truth and to know His will for our lives more fully. In this journey we are constantly "building on the foundation" of truth that has been laid down by faithful men and women of God who have gone before us.

Just as light dispels darkness, the truths of God's Word illuminate falsehoods we may have unknowingly embraced and cherished. The Christian life is one of constant growth. As the Holy Spirit leads us to humbly lay aside our preconceived opinions and with all of our hearts seek truth, God answers. As the prophet Jeremiah so aptly stated it, "You will seek Me and find Me, when you search for Me with all of your heart" (Jeremiah 29:13). An understanding of truth is as much a matter of the heart as it is the mind. When our hearts long to know truth and hunger for a clear revelation of God's will, He will reveal truth to us. This was certainly true of John Wesley.

God's light bearer

Centuries passed, and the light of truth in England flickered. Once again God's faithful followers faced fierce opposition. But God raised up two brothers, John and Charles Wesley, who would "contend for the faith" found in God's Word. Both of them struggled in their personal lives to discover a sense of the assurance of eternal life. They battled with feelings of inadequacy and a sense of lostness. Nothing they seemed to do was good enough. Their best efforts appeared worthless to assure them of salvation. Something was missing deep within. They depended on their good works for salvation but found their own efforts insufficient. When Charles developed a serious illness and it appeared that he might die, one of his friends asked what he based his hope of eternal life on. His response reveals his understanding of salvation at the time. It is reported that his comments went something like this: "Are not my good works a sufficient ground of my hope? I have nothing else to cling to." His mind was blinded to the salvation that there is in Christ.

The Wesley brothers did not yet grasp the salvation that Christ offers through faith. They were held captive to their own feeble efforts as the basis of salvation. They failed to understand that Christ's works alone atoned for their sins. His death satisfies the demands of a broken law. His righteousness alone is sufficient to merit salvation. His grace alone is sufficient to free us from the condemnation of the law.

Through the influence of a small group of Bible-believing Moravian Christians whose faith in Christ was unshakable, John and Charles came to the truth of the gospel. One day, John Wesley attended a Moravian meeting in London, where the leader of the group was reading from Luther's introduction to the letter to the Romans. John sat amazed at what he heard. For the first time in his life he began to understand the gospel. Something stirred within his soul. He felt himself strangely drawn to this Christ who had given His life for him. He experienced the dawn of new life deep within. Surprised by joy, he exclaimed, "I felt I did trust in Christ, Christ alone, for salvation: and an assurance was given me, that he had taken away my sins, even mine, and saved me from the law of sin and death."[4] After years of struggle, John Wesley discovered the Christ he had been seeking for decades. Once he discovered the matchless charms of Christ, he burned with the passion to share Jesus.

Like the apostle Paul, he joyously proclaimed, "For I am not ashamed of the gospel of Christ, for it is the power of God to salvation for everyone who believes, for the Jew first and also for the Greek. For in it the righteousness of God is revealed from faith to faith; as it is written, 'The just shall live by faith' " (Romans 1:16, 17). As the Wesleys preached Christ and Christ crucified, they continually experienced opposition. John was attacked by angry mobs, pelted with stones, and punched in the face; he escaped death on numerous occasions by miracles. The power of the Holy Spirit attended their work, and through their efforts more than a half million people were converted to Christ.

Law and grace harmonized

John Wesley saw the perfect harmony between the law and the gospel. Saved by grace, he longed to obey Christ. For Wesley, obedience was the fruit of faith. He understood that when Jesus declared, "I did not come to destroy the law but to fulfill it," Christ meant that He came to fill the law full of meaning. Jesus is the living law. He lived out the principles of the law in His life perfectly. He is our example. In His power and through His strength, we too are led to obedience.

After discussing salvation by faith and the futility of keeping the law in our own strength, Paul raises this question: "Do we then make void the law through faith? Certainly not! On the contrary, we establish the law" (Romans 3:31). In Romans 6:15, Paul makes it abundantly clear that grace in no way changes God's law. "What then? Shall we sin because we are not under the law but under grace? Certainly not!" According to the Bible, "sin is the transgression of the law" (1 John 3:4, KJV). So the apostle's question really is, "Shall we continue breaking the law because now we are no longer under its condemnation and are free in Christ?" His response is, "God forbid." John and Charles Wesley clearly understood that salvation by grace through faith did not give any individual the license to knowingly break God's law. Love always leads to obedience, and grace is always the power to obey.

In every generation God shed more and more light on His people. They hungered to understand more of His Word. They approached the Bible with a sense of reverence and excitement, believing that the same Holy

Spirit who inspired the Word in the first place would speak to them as they read it. Before opening the Bible, they prayed for divine guidance and believed God would speak to them through His Word. They approached the teachings of God's Word with the humility of a child, with an open mind and a receptive spirit.

As they prayerfully studied and meditated on the pages of Scripture, God revealed the wonders of His grace and the majesty of His love. They were willing to surrender any habit or attitude that God's Word revealed was not in harmony with His will and rejoiced that God was speaking to them personally through His inspired Word. God still speaks to us today through His Word. Its inspired pages still reveal His will for our lives. As you open its pages with an open mind and a prayerful heart, believing God will speak to you through His Word, you will be strangely warmed by His grace, charmed by His love, and transformed through His power.

1. William Tyndale, preface to *The Practice of Prelates*, 1531.

2. "What's Been Done, What's Left to Do," Wycliffe Bible Translators, October 2016, https://www.wycliffe.org.uk/wycliffe/about/statistics.html.

3. George Elwes Corrie, ed., *Sermons by Hugh Latimer, Sometime Bishop of Worcester, Martyr, 1555* (Cambridge, England: The University Press, 1844), xiii.

4. John Whitehead, *The Life of the Rev. John Wesley, M.A.* (London: Stephen Couchman, 1793), 331.

Chapter 7

A People of Destiny

As the disciples stood silently gazing into the sky to get their last lingering glimpse of their ascending Lord, suddenly two angels appeared in blazing glory. According to the divine record they stated, "Men of Galilee, why do you stand gazing up into heaven? This same Jesus, who was taken up from you into heaven, will so come in like manner as you have seen Him go into heaven" (Acts 1:10, 11).

A new sense of hope flooded into their minds. A new sense of joy burst upon their hearts. This same Jesus who walked the dusty streets of Galilee with them would one day return in glory. This same Jesus who healed the sick, opened blind eyes, unstopped deaf ears, loosed dumb tongues, and delivered ravaged bodies from life-threatening, debilitating sicknesses was coming again. This same Jesus who forgave adulterers, delivered demoniacs, pardoned sinners, and transformed Roman soldiers would return in glory. He would not forget them.

Faithful to His promise, Jesus would return. Had He

not encouraged them with these hopeful words: "Let not your heart be troubled; you believe in God, believe also in Me. In My Father's house are many mansions; if it were not so, I would have told you. I go to prepare a place for you. And if I go and prepare a place for you, I will come again" (John 14:1–3)? The promise of the return of our Lord has cheered the hearts of Christians for the past two thousand years. In times of deepest distress it has filled them with encouragement. In the times of persecution, facing death itself, they looked beyond the grave to the glorious return of our Lord. The apostle Paul calls the return of our Lord "the blessed hope."

Cheered by hope

What was it that cheered the faithful Waldenses in the midst of the horrible persecutions they faced? What gave Huss and Jerome, Tyndale and Latimer, and the martyrs of the Middle Ages the courage to face the flames and the sword? They looked beyond what was to what will be. They focused their thoughts beyond time to eternity. They believed that Christ had conquered the tomb, and one day Jesus would return as He promised and deliver them from the stranglehold of death. In the resurrection of Christ, death was a defeated foe. These courageous men and women clung to the promises of God's Word. They believed that "the Lord Himself will descend from heaven with a shout, with the voice of an archangel, and with the trumpet of God. And the dead in Christ will rise first. Then we who are alive and remain shall be caught up together with them in the clouds to meet the Lord in the air. And thus we shall always be with the

Lord" (1 Thessalonians 4:16, 17).

In the midst of their greatest trials, they clung to the hope of the return of our Lord. Their hearts pulsated with the desire to see Jesus come back in the clouds of glory. They recognized that death was a small matter in comparison to Christ's promise that one day, sickness, suffering, and sorrow would be gone forever, and they would live with Christ through all eternity.

The Advent hope revived

New Testament believers pulsated with the hope of Christ's soon return. The thought consumed them. They believed that He came once and was coming again. They believed that He would come literally, visibly, audibly, and gloriously to this world. To them, Christ's return was certainly not a secret or silent event. Revelation's predictions were too plain to be misunderstood. "He is coming with clouds, and every eye will see Him" (Revelation 1:7). John the Revelator adds, "Then the seventh angel sounded; and there were loud voices in heaven, saying, 'The kingdoms of this world have become the kingdoms of our Lord and of His Christ, and He shall reign forever and ever' " (Revelation 11:15). Revelation 19 reveals that Jesus is coming "in righteousness" as "King of kings and Lord of lords." These promises from God's Word have filled the hearts of believers with hope down through the centuries.

Yet as time passed for many of these Christians, this hope grew dim. Time passed. Christ did not come, and their faith waned. The things of time crowded out the things of eternity. As the years stretched into decades and centuries passed, some church scholars even began to teach that the coming of Christ was not His coming in glory but rather a spiritualized coming, when He comes into our hearts. One of the early church fathers, Origen, taught this spiritualized view of the coming of Christ. His understanding was that Christ returned when His Spirit entered a believer's life. In the fifth century A.D. Augustine taught that the millennial reign of Christ began with the creation of Christ's church at His first coming. With these unscriptural views of the second coming of Christ, the church largely lost its passion about our Lord's return. The urgency of personally preparing for Christ's coming and warning the world of His return faded into insignificance. Centuries passed with little emphasis on this central Bible truth.

Light shines from the Word

In the late 1700s and early 1800s, the light of the Advent truth shined brightly upon conscientious students of Scripture who were longing to understand Bible prophecy better. As they pored over the Scriptures, they observed that the second coming of our Lord is mentioned fifteen hundred times in the Bible. The New Testament mentions it more than three hundred times, or once in every twenty-five verses. These faithful Bible students began studying the prophecies of the prophetic books of Daniel and Revelation.

God often moves upon the hearts of men and women in concert in different parts of the world to discover and disseminate Bible truths that were lost sight of for centuries. At a time when the majority of Christian leaders neglected the study of Bible prophecy and believed that the coming of Christ's kingdom was the millennial reign of Christ on earth, God began moving upon the hearts of diligent Bible students. They spent days poring over the prophecies of Scripture. They were deeply moved by the thought that Christ was coming soon.

While serving as the pastor of a church on the outskirts of Frankfurt, Germany, from 1746 to 1792, Pastor Johann Petri began studying and writing on Daniel's prophecies. Petri believed the time periods of Daniel revealed that the coming of Christ was near. Johann Bengel, who lived fifty years before Petri, was also convinced on the basis of his study of prophecy that Christ was coming soon. A Jesuit priest, Manual Lacunza, studied the Second Advent and the prophecies of Scripture for twenty years. He believed that the two advents of Christ were the focal points of human history. He secretly wrote a tract under the pseudonym Juan Josafat Ben-Ezra, or Rabbi Ben Ezra. Lacunza recognized that since his conclusions were diametrically opposed to the state church and would incur the wrath of the authorities, it was more prudent to write under an assumed name. The booklet he wrote titled, "The Coming of the Messiah in Glory and Majesty" influenced an entire generation of biblical scholars.

The truth of the coming of Jesus brought revival to the church in the late 1700s and early 1800s. Clear messages on the return of our Lord rang out from pulpits throughout Europe. One of the strongest centers for preaching the second coming of Christ was the British Isles. Two men stand out particularly: Joseph Wolff and Edward

Irving. Joseph Wolff was the son of a Jewish rabbi. At a very early age he had serious questions about Jesus' identity as the world's true Messiah. On one occasion he was talking to a Christian neighbor who challenged him to read Isaiah 53. Young Joseph took up the challenge and was convinced that the prophecy found its fulfillment in Jesus of Nazareth. When he asked his father to explain Isaiah 53, he was met with stern resistance and told never to mention the topic again. This only increased his desire to know more about Jesus of Nazareth.

Over time, as he continued to study, Joseph Wolff fully accepted Christ as his personal Savior, and he, too, was drawn to a study of the prophecies of the second coming of Christ. While he taught that salvation came only through the death of Christ on Calvary's cross, he powerfully preached a message of preparation for the return of Christ. On one occasion he wrote, "Jesus of Nazareth, the true Messiah, whose hands and feet were pierced, who was brought like a lamb to the slaughter, who was the man of sorrows and acquainted with grief, who after the scepter was taken from Judah, and the legislative power from between His feet, came the first time; shall come the second time in the clouds of heaven, and with the trump of the Archangel."[1]

Joseph Wolff's gift for languages made him an ideal "missionary to the world." He spoke six languages fluently and conversed freely in another eight. He traversed the burning desert sands of Asia, preaching to Jews, Muslims, Hindus, and Parses. As he traveled in barbarous lands without the protection of any European governments, he endured hardships, experienced difficulties, and faced death on numerous occasions. He was robbed, captured, sold as a slave, and sometimes nearly perished from thirst in the desert. One time he was robbed of all his possessions and forced to travel on foot in the snow through horrible conditions—nearly freezing to death. What prompted him to give up the pleasures of home, the comforts of family and friends, to travel endlessly to distant lands? There was only one thing. He passionately believed that Christ was coming soon and the world needed to know the way of eternal life through Jesus Christ, our Lord.

In 1837, Wolff was invited to speak to the American Congress, where once again he shared his belief that the world must know the message of the soon return of our Lord.

God was moving on hearts all over the world and raising up men and women to herald the truth regarding the return of Jesus. Not all of them understood the biblical teaching clearly, but these misunderstandings did not keep them from enthusiastically proclaiming the truth about Jesus' coming in the clouds of heaven. There was one common thread that ran through all of their messages: the necessity of preparing for the soon return of Christ in glory in the clouds of heaven.

Edward Irving and three hundred preachers of the Church of England heralded the second coming of Jesus powerfully throughout the British Isles. Every week Irving taught the nearness of Christ's return before packed congregations of a thousand people in his London church. In Scotland, he preached to crowds of up to twelve thousand in the open air. Irving's oratory skills, enthusiastic preaching, biblical knowledge, and deep piety deeply moved his audiences to repent of their sins and prepare for the coming of their Lord.

The father of the modern Advent movement

One man who might be called the father of this modern Advent movement was William Miller. Born in 1782, Miller was brought up in a religious home. His mother was a godly woman who taught her son the importance of honesty, thrift, and perseverance. He was taught to work hard at an early age on the family farm. As he grew to manhood he continued as a farmer but also held offices as a justice of the peace and deputy sheriff. He served in the 30th Infantry Regiment in the War of 1812 as a captain in the army. The war had a great impact on this thoughtful young soldier. He saw death up close, and the sight of his comrades lying on the battlefield with bullet holes in their heads awakened within him thoughts of eternity.

When he returned from the war-torn battlefields, he began searching for meaning and purpose in his life. Miller was greatly influenced by a group of men who were upright citizens and influential thought leaders in his community. These deists, as they were called, believed that God existed on the basis of reason alone, but they rejected belief in a supernatural deity who interacts with mankind. To them the Bible was for unthinking, ignorant people. They believed the miracles of Scripture were conjured-up myths and prayer was psychological nonsense.

Accepting this worldview left William Miller hopeless. He put it this way: "Annihilation was a cold and chilling thought, and accountability was sure destruction to all. The heavens were as brass over my head, and the earth as iron under my feet. Eternity! What was it? And death, why was it?"[2] From time to time, although in a desperate spiritual state himself, Miller was asked to read the local preacher's sermons when the itinerant preacher was away. One Sunday as he was reading the prepared text, he became so overwhelmed with emotion he could not continue and left the pulpit. The seeds of faith were growing in his heart. The sunshine of God's love was shining into his darkened mind. Hope was dawning in his soul.

Christ breaks through

As he continued to study Scripture, Miller found a Christ who atoned for his sins. He discovered a Savior who provided pardon, freedom from guilt, and the power to live a new life. Christ was everything his aching heart needed. In Jesus, he found a friend—One whose love would never let him go and whose grace provided for his heart's needs. The Savior became to him the "chiefest among ten thousand" and the Bible a most precious guide for his life. He spent hours, days, and weeks studying Scripture. When he did not understand a passage, he compared it with other passages until its meaning became clear. He laid aside all of his preconceived opinions and compared scripture with scripture. He began with the Bible's first book, Genesis, and methodically examined each Bible text in light of other texts on the same topic. When he came to the prophecies of Daniel and Revelation, he used this same method of careful study.

Gradually the truth of our Lord's second advent dawned upon his mind. As he studied the numerous passages on Christ's return to earth, he came to the conclusion that

Christ was coming in power and glory before the thousand years in heaven (Revelation 20:4). Numerous Bible students around the world were coming to this same conclusion. The more he studied, the more Miller was convinced that Jesus was not only coming in glory to this world but also that He was coming soon. The urgency of the return of Christ burned in his heart. This sense of the nearness of our Lord's return moved him to the core of his being.

Eventually he came to the conclusion through his study of the prophecies of Daniel that Christ would return in or around 1843 or 1844. When the invitation came to share his convictions with others, Miller felt compelled to explain the end-time prophecies that had become the passion of his life. Spiritual revivals broke out almost everywhere he preached. Hearts were touched. Lives were changed. People by the thousands were converted in his prophetic-preaching meetings. Those who accepted his message were led to a sense of deep repentance before God, and their lives were changed.

Although he faced fierce opposition by some and was considered a wild-eyed fanatic by others, the fruits of his labors revealed a divine imprint upon his ministry. When Christ did not appear at the time these early Adventists expected Him to, William Miller and his associates were ridiculed, mocked, and scorned. After this great disappointment, a friend asked Miller when he now expected Christ to come. His response: "I have fixed my mind on another time and it is today and today and today."

For each one of us, William Miller's words are timely. The only way to be ready for the return of our Lord is to get ready today and stay ready until He comes. If today is the last day of our lives, the next event that we will experience if we have been faithful to Christ is the coming of our Lord. Christ earnestly appeals to us to live in expectation of the coming of Jesus daily and to prepare for His return as if it would happen today.

Disappointment fades, hope dawns

For a moment let your mind drift back over the centuries to the horrible events of the crucifixion that Friday afternoon. The disciples were bitterly disappointed. They thought Jesus was going to deliver them from the yoke of Roman bondage, but now He was dead. Their hopes were dashed. Their joy danced away like a shadow. The bloody, mangled body of Christ hanging on the cross brought deep grief to their hearts. They felt hopeless—hopeless, that is, until that glorious Sunday morning when Christ rose from the dead. Out of the disappointment of A.D. 31 God raised up the New Testament church to impact the world with the life-changing message of Christ. Would God once again bring joy out of sorrow, hope out of despair, and light out of darkness?

The great prophecies of the Bible's closing book reveal a divine movement of destiny arising out of disappointment to proclaim God's last-day message to the world. Revelation 14 describes a worldwide movement spanning the globe with the good news of the eternal gospel. It reveals a last-day message calling all men and women to "fear God and give glory to Him, for the hour of His judgment has come; and worship Him who made heaven and earth, the sea and springs of water" (Revelation 14:7).

In an age of belief in evolution, God's final message

calls all people everywhere to worship their Creator. The very basis for worship is that God is our Creator. Revelation 4:11 declares, "You are worthy, O Lord, to receive glory and honor and power; for You created all things, and by Your will they exist and were created." All true worship flows out of a heart of deep gratitude. We did not evolve. We are not some advanced protein molecule or a genetic accident. We were fashioned, shaped, and created by God. Creation is a constant reminder that life's deepest purpose is to worship the God who made us. This is precisely why God's last-day message for humanity includes an urgent appeal to "worship Him who made heaven and earth, the sea and springs of water." This is precisely why He has given us the seventh-day Sabbath as a memorial of His creative power and authority (Genesis 2:1–3; Exodus 20:8–11; Ezekiel 20:12).

The Sabbath commandment in the heart of God's Law was lost sight of by the majority of Christians for centuries. Although there always have been a few faithful believers whose consciences were shaped by the Word of God and have kept the Sabbath, most Christians mistakenly assumed that the Sabbath was done away with at the Cross.

To complete the Reformation, God has raised up a last-day people to stand on the shoulders of the great Reformers of the past with the Bible as their only creed, Christ alone as their source of salvation, the Holy Spirit as their only source of strength, and the return of our Lord as the consummation of all their hopes. John describes this group of Bible-believing Christians when he says, "Here is the patience of the saints; here are those who keep the commandments of God and the faith of

Jesus" (Revelation 14:12). Truths long obscured by the darkness of error and tradition, including the true Bible Sabbath, would be discovered and proclaimed to the world just before the return of our Lord. God's people are identified as a body of Christ-centered believers filled with the faith of Jesus who lovingly keep His commandments, including the Bible Sabbath. Seventh-day Adventists have been providentially raised up by God as a Bible-believing, Christ-centered movement to complete the Reformation. They stand for the truths of Scripture, long lost sight of through the centuries, including the urgency of preparing for the soon return of Jesus and the enduring symbol of Creation, the Bible Sabbath. Like the Reformers before them, Seventh-day Adventists have taken a stand on unpopular truths of Scripture.

The Reformation continues today. It did not stop with the deaths of the Reformers. God had more truth to reveal. Just as He called men and women from the comfortable convenience of popular religion in the Middle Ages, He is calling all peoples everywhere today to make eternal decisions to follow His truth. Are you willing to say deep within your heart, "Jesus, wherever You lead, I will follow"? Are you willing to declare your allegiance to Christ and the eternal truths of His Word? Will you say, "Jesus, I am Yours today; through Your power and by Your grace, I will follow Your truth now and forever"?

---

1. Joseph Wolff, *Researches and Missionary Labours* (Philadelphia: Orrin Rogers, 1837), 51, 52.

2. Joshua V. Himes, *Views of the Prophecies and Prophetic Chronology Selected From Manuscripts of William Miller* (Boston: Joshua V. Himes, 1842), 10.

FREE Lessons at www.BibleStudies.com

Call:
1-888-456-7933

Write:
Discover
P.O. Box 999
Loveland, CO 80539-0999

It's easy to learn more about the Bible!